GRADE
4

Common CORE Writing

MW01233382

Table of Contents

Introduction

What Is the Common Core?

The Common Core State Standards are an initiative by states to set shared, consistent, and clear expectations of what students are expected to learn. This helps teachers and parents know what they need to do to help students. The standards are designed to be rigorous and pertinent to the real world. They reflect the knowledge and skills that young people need for success in college and careers.

If your state has joined the Common Core State Standards Initiative, then teachers are required to incorporate these standards into their lesson plans. Students need targeted practice in order to meet grade-level standards and expectations, and thereby be promoted to the next grade.

What Does It Mean to Write to Texts?

One of the most important instructional shifts in the Common Core State Standards is writing to texts, or sources. What exactly does this mean? Haven't standardized assessments always used reading texts as a springboard to writing? Yes, but the required writing hasn't always been DEPENDENT on the key ideas and details in a text.

A prompt that is non-text-dependent asks students to rely on prior knowledge or experience. In fact, students could likely carry out the writing without reading the text at all. The writing does not need to include ideas, information, and key vocabulary from the text.

Writing to texts requires students to analyze, clarify, and cite information they read in the text. The writing reveals whether students have performed a close reading, because it is designed to elicit ideas, information, and key vocabulary from the text as well as students' own evidence-based inferences and conclusions. These are all skills that prepare them for the grades ahead, college, the workplace, and real-world applications in their adult daily lives.

An example of a passage with non-text-dependent and text-dependent sample prompts is provided on page 3.

Simple and Compound Machines

1. A simple machine is a tool that does work with one movement. Like all machines, a simple machine makes work easier. It has few or no moving parts and uses energy to do work. A lever, a wedge, a screw, a pulley, a wheel and axle, and an inclined plane are all simple machines.

2. You use simple machines all the time, too. If you have ever played on a seesaw or walked up a ramp, then you have used a simple machine. If you have opened a door, eaten with a spoon, cut with scissors, or zipped up a zipper, you have used a simple machine.

3. A compound machine is made of two or more simple machines. For example, the pedals, wheels, and gears on a bicycle are wheels and axles, and the hand brakes on the handlebars are levers. Cars, airplanes, watches, and washing machines are also examples of compound machines. Compound machines are very useful because they can do the work of many simple machines at the same time.

4. Life would be very different if we did not have machines. Work would be much harder, and playing wouldn't be as much fun.

Standard	Sample Prompt: Non-Text-Dependent	Sample Prompt: Text Dependent
W.4.1 (Opinion/ Argument)	Do you prefer zippers, buttons, buckles, or another type of fastener for your clothing? Why?	The author makes three claims in the last paragraph. Choose one of the claims, tell whether you agree or disagree, and support your opinion with evidence from the text.
W.4.2 (Informative/ Explanatory)	Think about a machine you have used to do a task. How did you use it? How did using the machine make the task easier?	Compare and contrast simple and compound machines. Use details from the text to support your explanation.
W.4.3 (Narrative)	Write a story in which a character invents a machine that no one has seen or heard of before.	Imagine that all the machines mentioned in the passage disappeared for twenty-four hours. Write a journal entry about how your life was different that day and what you learned.

Using This Book

How Does This Book Help Students?

This book is organized into four main sections: Writing Mini-Lessons, Practice Texts with Prompts, Graphic Organizers and Checklists, and Rubrics and Assessments. All mini-lessons and practice pages are self-contained and may be used in any order that meets the needs of students. The elements of this book work together to provide students with the tools they need to be able to master the range of skills and application as required by the Common Core.

1. Mini-Lessons for Opinion/Argument, Informative/Explanatory, and Narrative Writing

Writing mini-lessons prepare students to use writing as a way to state and support opinions, demonstrate understanding of the subjects they are studying, and convey real and imagined experiences. The mini-lessons are organized in the order of the standards, but you may wish to do them with your class in an order that matches your curriculum. For each type of writing the first mini-lesson covers responding to one text, while the second mini-lesson models how to respond to multiple texts.

Each mini-lesson begins with a lesson plan that provides step-by-step instruction.

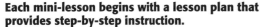
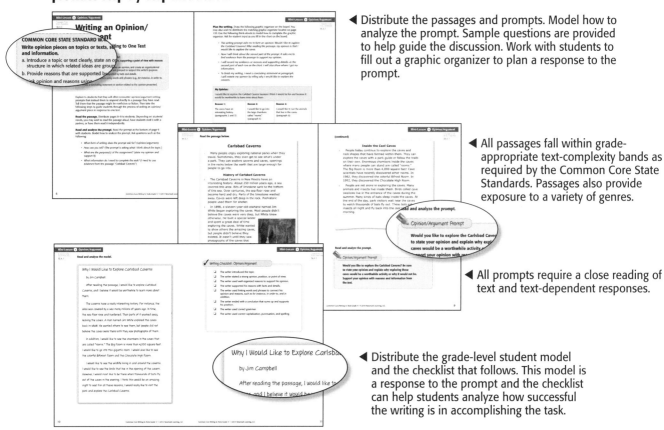

◄ Distribute the passages and prompts. Model how to analyze the prompt. Sample questions are provided to help guide the discussion. Work with students to fill out a graphic organizer to plan a response to the prompt.

◄ All passages fall within grade-appropriate text-complexity bands as required by the Common Core State Standards. Passages also provide exposure to a variety of genres.

◄ All prompts require a close reading of text and text-dependent responses.

◄ Distribute the grade-level student model and the checklist that follows. This model is a response to the prompt and the checklist can help students analyze how successful the writing is in accomplishing the task.

Common Core Writing to Texts Grade 4 • ©2014 Newmark Learning, LLC

2. Practice Texts with Prompts

Passages and prompts provide students with real experience writing to a single text and multiple texts. The first ten lessons require students to respond to one text. The last ten require students to respond to multiple texts.

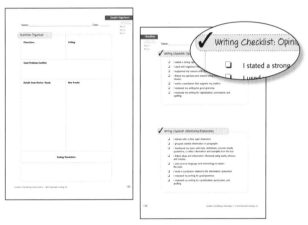

Each passage or pair of passages is followed by three text-dependent prompts: Opinion/Argument, Informative/Explanatory, and Narrative. You may wish to assign a particular prompt, have students choose one, or have them execute each type of writing over a longer period of time.

For more information on how to use this section, see page 48.

3. Graphic Organizers and Checklists

For each type of writing, you can distribute a corresponding graphic organizer and checklist to help students plan and evaluate their writing. A chart with editing and proofreading marks can also be found on page 136 if you choose to have students work though the full editing and revising process.

4. Rubrics and Assessments

The section includes Evaluation Rubrics to guide your assessment and scoring of students' responses. Based on your observations of students' writing, use the differentiated rubrics. These are designed to help you conduct meaningful conferences with students and will help differentiate your interactions to match students' needs.

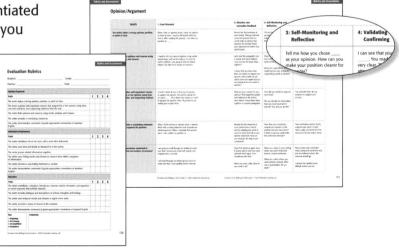

For each score a student receives in the Evaluation Rubrics, responsive prompts are provided. These gradual-release prompts scaffold writers toward mastery of each writing type.

COMMON CORE
STATE STANDARD
W.4.1

Writing an Opinion/ Argument

Mini-Lesson 1: Writing to One Text

> **COMMON CORE STATE STANDARD W.4.1**
>
> **Write opinion pieces on topics or texts, supporting a point of view with reasons and information.**
>
> a. Introduce a topic or text clearly, state an opinion, and create an organizational structure in which related ideas are grouped to support the writer's purpose.
>
> b. Provide reasons that are supported by facts and details.
>
> c. Link opinion and reasons using words and phrases (e.g., *for instance, in order to, in addition*).
>
> d. Provide a concluding statement or section related to the opinion presented.

Explain to students that they will often encounter opinion/argument writing prompts that instruct them to respond directly to a passage they have read. Tell them that the passage might be nonfiction or fiction. Then take the following steps to guide students through the process of writing an opinion/ argument piece in response to one text.

Read the passage. Distribute pages 8–9 to students. Depending on students' needs, you may wish to read the passage aloud, have students read it with a partner, or have them read it independently.

Read and analyze the prompt. Read the prompt at the bottom of page 9 with students. Model how to analyze the prompt. Ask questions such as the following:

- *What form of writing does the prompt ask for?* (opinion/argument)

- *How can you tell?* (The prompt is asking what I think about the topic.)

- *What is the purpose of the assignment?* (state my opinion and support it)

- *What information do I need to complete the task?* (I need to use evidence from the passage "Carlsbad Caverns.")

COMMON CORE
STATE STANDARD
W.4.1

Plan the writing. Draw the following graphic organizer on the board. You may also wish to distribute the matching graphic organizer located on page 120. Use the following think-alouds to model how to complete the graphic organizer. Ask for student input as you fill in the chart on the board.

- *The writing prompt asks me to form an opinion. Would I like to explore the Carlsbad Caverns? After reading the passage, my opinion is that I would like to explore the caves.*

- *Now I will think about the second part of the prompt. It asks me to find evidence from the passage to support my opinion.*

- *I will record my evidence—or reasons and supporting details—in the second part of each column on the chart. I will also show where I got my information.*

- *To finish my writing, I need a concluding statement or paragraph. I will restate my opinion by telling why I would like to explore the caverns.*

My Opinion:

I would like to explore the Carlsbad Caverns because I think it would be fun and because it would be worthwhile to learn more about them.

Reason 1:	**Reason 2:**	**Reason 3:**
The caves have an interesting history. (paragraphs 2 and 3)	I would like to go into the large chambers called rooms. (paragraph 5)	I would like to see the animals that live in the caves. (paragraph 6)
Supporting Details: 1. The area was once covered by a sea. 2. Prehistoric people used the caves for shelter. 3. A man named Jim White began exploring them in 1898.	**Supporting Details:** 1. The Big Room is more than 4,000 square feet. 2. The Bifrost Room is colorful. 3. The Chocolate High Room is a recent discovery.	**Supporting Details:** 1. Birds live in the entrance to the caves. 2. Thousands of bats fly out of the caves each evening.

My Opinion Restated (Conclusion):

I think I would really enjoy exploring the caves and learning more about them.

Read and analyze the model. Distribute the student writing model and checklist on pages 10–11 to students. Read them aloud. Discuss with students whether or not the writer was successful at accomplishing the task. Ask them to complete the checklist as you discuss the opinion/argument piece.

COMMON CORE
STATE STANDARD
W.4.1

Read the passage below.

Carlsbad Caverns

1.   Many people enjoy exploring national parks when they travel. Sometimes, they even get to see what's under a park. They can explore caverns and caves, openings in the rocks below the earth that are large enough for people to go into.

History of Carlsbad Caverns

2.   The Carlsbad Caverns in New Mexico have an interesting history. About 250 million years ago, a sea covered this area. Bits of limestone sank to the bottom of this sea. Over centuries, the sea floor rose and became hard and dry. Parts of the limestone washed away. Caves were left deep in the rock. Prehistoric people used them for shelter.

3.   In 1898, a sixteen-year-old cowhand named Jim White began exploring the caves. Most people didn't believe the caves were very deep, but White knew otherwise. He built a special ladder and spent a great deal of time exploring the caves. White wanted to show others the amazing caves, but people didn't believe they existed. It wasn't until they saw photographs of the caves that people began exploring them. Early visitors were lowered down into the caves in large buckets using ropes and pulleys.

4.   In 1930, the area became a national park. Stairs were built and electric lights and elevators were installed in the caves. White spent most of his life exploring the caves and even became involved in overseeing their care and protection.

(continued)

(continued)

Inside the Cool Caves

5.   People today continue to explore the caves and rock shapes that have formed within them. They can explore the caves with a park guide or follow the trails on their own. Enormous chambers inside the caves where many people can stand are called rooms. The Big Room is more than 4,000 square feet! Cave scientists have recently discovered other rooms. In 1982, they discovered the colorful Bifrost Room. In 1992, they discovered the Chocolate High Room.

6.   People are not alone in exploring the caves. Many animals and insects live inside them. Birds called cave swallows live in the entrance of the caves during the summer. Many kinds of bats sleep inside the caves. At the end of the day, park visitors wait near the caves to watch thousands of bats fly out. These bats eat insects all night and fly back into the cool caves in the morning.

Read and analyze the prompt.

Opinion/Argument Prompt

Would you like to explore the Carlsbad Caverns? Be sure to state your opinion and explain why exploring these caves would be a worthwhile activity or why it would not be. Support your opinion with reasons and information from the text.

COMMON CORE
STATE STANDARD
W.4.1

Read and analyze the model.

Why I Would Like to Explore Carlsbad Caverns

by Jim Campbell

After reading the passage, I would like to explore Carlsbad Caverns, and I believe it would be worthwhile to learn more about them.

The caverns have a really interesting history. For instance, the area was covered by a sea many millions of years ago. In time, the sea floor rose and hardened. Then parts of it washed away, leaving the caves. A man named Jim White explored the caves back in 1898. He wanted others to see them, but people did not believe the caves were there until they saw photographs of them.

In addition, I would like to see the chambers in the caves that are called rooms. The Big Room is more than 4,000 square feet. I would like to go into this gigantic room. I would also like to see the colorful Bifrost Room and the Chocolate High Room.

I would like to see the wildlife living in and around the caverns. I would like to see the birds that live in the opening of the cavern. However, I would most like to be there when thousands of bats fly out of the caves in the evening. I think this would be an amazing sight to see! For all these reasons, I would really like to visit the park and explore the Carlsbad Caverns.

Common Core Writing to Texts Grade 4 • ©2014 Newmark Learning, LLC

COMMON CORE
STATE STANDARD
W.4.1

✔ Writing Checklist: Opinion/Argument

❏   The writer introduced the topic.

❏   The writer stated a strong opinion, position, or point of view.

❏   The writer used well-organized reasons to support his opinion.

❏   The writer supported his reasons with facts and details.

❏   The writer used linking words and phrases to connect his opinion and reasons, such as *for instance, in order to,* and *in addition.*

❏   The writer ended with a conclusion that sums up and supports his position.

❏   The writer used correct grammar.

❏   The writer used correct capitalization, punctuation, and spelling.

COMMON CORE
STATE STANDARD
W.4.1

Writing an Opinion/ Argument

Mini-Lesson 2: Writing to Multiple Texts

COMMON CORE STATE STANDARD W.4.1

Write opinion pieces on topics or texts, supporting a point of view with reasons and information.

a. Introduce a topic or text clearly, state an opinion, and create an organizational structure in which related ideas are grouped to support the writer's purpose.

b. Provide reasons that are supported by facts and details.

c. Link opinion and reasons using words and phrases (e.g., *for instance, in order to, in addition*).

d. Provide a concluding statement or section related to the opinion presented.

Explain to students that they will often encounter writing prompts that instruct them to respond directly to more than one passage. For example, they might have to read two informational passages about the same topic or two fiction passages by the same author. Then take the following steps to guide students through the process of writing an opinion/argument in response to multiple texts.

Read the passages. Distribute pages 14–17 to students. Depending on students' needs, you may wish to read the passages aloud, have students read them with a partner, or have them read the passages independently.

Read and analyze the prompt. Read the prompt at the bottom of page 17 with students. Model how to analyze the prompt. Ask questions such as the following:

- *What form of writing does the prompt ask for?* (opinion/argument)

- *How can you tell?* (The prompt is asking what I think about the topic.)

- *What is the purpose of the assignment?* (state my opinion and support it)

- *What information do I need to complete the task?* (I need to use evidence from both "Orangutans" and "Chimpanzees.")

COMMON CORE
STATE STANDARD
W.4.1

Plan the writing. Draw the following graphic organizer on the board. You may also wish to distribute the matching graphic organizer located on page 121. Use the following think-alouds to model how to complete the graphic organizer. Ask for student input as you fill in the chart.

- *The writing prompt asks me to form an opinion. After reading both passages, I think our class should research more about chimpanzees because of how they live together in communities and get along with one another.*

- *Now I will think about the second part of the prompt. It asks me to find evidence from both "Orangutans" and "Chimpanzees" to support my opinion.*

- *I will record my evidence—or reasons and supporting details—in the last three rows of the chart.*

- *To finish my writing, I need a concluding statement or paragraph. I will restate my opinion by explaining why our class should learn more about chimpanzees rather than orangutans.*

My Opinion: Our science class should learn more about chimpanzees because of how they live together in communities and get along with one another.	
Text 1: "Orangutans"	**Text 2:** "Chimpanzees"
Reason 1: Orangutans are solitary apes.	**Reason 1:** Chimps live together in communities.
Supporting Evidence: 1. Orangutans prefer to live alone. 2. The only exceptions are young orangutans; they stay with their mothers for many years.	**Supporting Evidence:** 1. Families of chimpanzees live together in communities. 2. Young chimps within a community play together. 3. Members of a community sleep in nests near each other.
Reason 2: Orangutans don't like to be with other orangutans.	**Reason 2:** Chimps like to be together.
Supporting Evidence: 1. Males make loud calls to warn other males to stay away.	**Supporting Evidence:** 1. They groom each other. 2. They greet each other with a hug or pat on the back.
My Conclusion: I think our science class would enjoy learning more about chimpanzees. The way they socialize and interact makes them more interesting than orangutans.	

Read and analyze the model. Distribute the student writing model and checklist on pages 18–19 to students. Read it aloud. Discuss with students whether or not the writer was successful at accomplishing the task. Ask them to complete the checklist as you discuss the opinion/argument piece.

COMMON CORE
STATE STANDARD

W.4.1

Read the passages.

Orangutans

1. Orangutans are enormous apes with reddish-orange hair. They are known for their large size and high intelligence. Orangutans live only in the rain forests of Sumatra and Borneo, two islands in Southeast Asia.

Size

2. Orangutans live mostly in trees. They rarely stand on the ground, but if they do, they are about 4 feet (1.2 meters) tall and can weigh up to 200 pounds (91 kilograms). Orangutans have exceptionally long arms. If an orangutan stretches out its arms, the length of its arms from fingertips to fingertips might be more than 7 feet (2 meters). Such large arms enable orangutans to easily swing from branch to branch and make their way through the forest.

Intelligence

3. Scientists believe that orangutans are extremely intelligent. They sometimes make tools to help them eat. For example, they create a spoonlike device to scoop out and eat seeds from the inside of fruit. To stay dry, orangutans use large leaves like an umbrella. They also use leaves as cups to drink water. Orangutans in zoos have been smart enough to use a touch screen on a computer! They have even been known to play video games.

(continued)

(continued)

Diet

4. Orangutans are omnivores. This means that they eat both plants and meat. They eat mainly tropical fruit but also leaves, bark, and insects. Scientists have recorded orangutans eating more than 400 different foods.

Social Habits

5. Orangutans usually live alone instead of with other orangutans. Scientists think this is because a single orangutan needs a great deal of food. Baby orangutans are the exception to this rule. It isn't uncommon for a baby orangutan to stay with its mother for seven or more years. Male orangutans can make loud, long calls that can be heard from almost a mile away! Males most often do this to warn other males to stay away. Orangutans are generally shy and prefer to stay away from people.

Fast Facts About Orangutans

Appearance:	large head and cheek flaps, very long arms, no tail; reddish-orange fur; dark face
Size:	between 3 and 4.5 feet (.9 and 1.4 meters) tall; males are larger than females
Weight:	between 110 and 200 pounds (50 and 91 kilograms); males are heavier than females
Habitat:	tropical rain forests of Sumatra and Borneo
Diet:	omnivores: eat fruit, leaves, bark, insects, and meat
Behavior:	solitary: prefer to live alone
Life Span:	about 35 years in the wild, much longer in captivity

(continue to next passage)

(continued)

Chimpanzees

1.   Chimpanzees, or chimps, are small, social apes. Chimps have long, black hair, and their faces are usually pink. They have large ears and small nostrils. A chimp can make expressions like a person to show when the chimp is happy, excited, fearful, or angry. Although they normally walk on all fours, chimps can also stand on two legs and walk upright. Chimps are fairly small apes; they stand between 2 and 4 feet (.6 and 1.2 meters) tall and weigh between 60 and 120 pounds (27 and 54 kilograms). They live throughout western and central Africa.

Communication

2.   Chimps are extremely social and prefer to be in the company of other chimps. They communicate with one another using hand gestures and by grunting, barking, and even screaming. A chimp will greet another chimp with a hug or a pat on the back. When a group of chimps discovers a large supply of food, the chimps will swing through the trees making loud noises and pounding on tree trunks. This alerts other chimps of the discovery.

Communities

3.   Chimp families live together in communities. About fifty chimps make up a community, which consists of several families. Young chimps within a community play together. All members of the community spend time grooming, or cleaning, one another's hair. Chimps spend some time on the ground, but they eat and sleep in trees. Each evening, a chimp will build a nest to sleep in. This nest is shaped like a bowl and is made of leaves and other plants. Members of a community build their nests near one another.

(continued)

(continued)

Common Core
State Standard
W.4.1

Intelligence

4.   Chimpanzees are extremely intelligent and create and use simple tools. For example, a chimp will use chewed leaves as a sponge to soak up water to drink. It will use sticks to dig insects out of logs and stones to break open nuts. Chimps are capable of learning difficult tasks. Chimps in captivity have been taught to communicate with people using sign language. A chimpanzee named Lana learned to press symbols on a computer keyboard to create sentences asking for food, a drink, and even music.

Fast Facts About Chimpanzees

Appearance:	thick body, long arms, no tail; long, black hair; pink or tan face
Size:	between 2 and 4 feet (.6 and 1.2 meters) tall; males are taller than females
Weight:	between 60 and 120 pounds (27 and 54 kilograms); males are heavier than females
Habitat:	prefer the dense, tropical rain forests in Africa
Diet:	omnivores; eat leaves, fruit, seeds, bark, insects, eggs, meat, and other foods
Behavior:	social, live together in communities
Life Span:	about 50 years in the wild, longer in captivity

Read and analyze the prompt.

Opinion/Argument Prompt

Imagine that your science teacher tells your class it can choose to research either orangutans or chimpanzees. After reading the passages, which group do you think your class should learn more about? Why? Use details from both "Orangutans" and "Chimpanzees" in your answer.

COMMON CORE
STATE STANDARD
W.4.1

Read and analyze the model.

Why We Should Learn More About Chimpanzees

by Anna Connelly

I think our science class should learn more about chimpanzees because it is interesting how chimps live together and get along with one another.

Families of chimpanzees live together in communities. These are large groups of chimpanzees. A community might consist of several chimpanzee families. Based on the passage, members of a community spend a lot of time together. Young chimpanzees in a community play together, and members of a community sleep near one another in nests at night. Orangutans, on the other hand, prefer to live alone. They spend their lives in trees and do not like to be with other orangutans.

In addition, it's very interesting how chimpanzees interact with and get along with one another. The passage says that they spend time grooming one another. It also says that they greet one another with a hug or a pat on the back and "talk" to one another by grunting, barking, and sometimes yelling. Male orangutans, on the other hand, only make loud calls to warn other male orangutans to stay away.

For these reasons, I think our science class would enjoy learning more about chimpanzees. The way they socialize and interact makes them more interesting than orangutans.

COMMON CORE
STATE STANDARD
W.4.1

✔ Writing Checklist: Opinion/Argument

❏ The writer introduced the topic.

❏ The writer stated a strong opinion, position, or point of view.

❏ The writer used well-organized reasons from both passages to support her opinion.

❏ The writer supported her reasons with facts and details.

❏ The writer used linking words and phrases to connect her opinion and reasons, such as *for instance, in order to,* and *in addition.*

❏ The writer ended with a conclusion that sums up and supports her position.

❏ The writer used correct grammar.

❏ The writer used correct capitalization, punctuation, and spelling.

COMMON CORE
STATE STANDARD
W.4.2

Writing an Informative/ Explanatory Text

Mini-Lesson 3: **Writing to One Text**

> **COMMON CORE STATE STANDARD W.4.2**
>
> **Write informative/explanatory texts to examine a topic and convey ideas and information clearly.**
>
> a. Introduce a topic clearly and group related information in paragraphs and sections; include formatting (e.g., headings), illustrations, and multimedia when useful to aiding comprehension.
>
> b. Develop the topic with facts, definitions, concrete details, quotations, or other information and examples related to the topic.
>
> c. Link ideas within categories of information using words and phrases (e.g., *another, for example, also, because*).
>
> d. Use precise language and domain-specific vocabulary to inform about or explain the topic.
>
> e. Provide a concluding statement or section related to the information or explanation presented.

Explain to students that they will often encounter informative/explanatory writing prompts that instruct them to respond directly to a passage they have read. Tell them that the passage might be nonfiction or fiction. Then take the following steps to guide students through the process of informative/ explanatory writing in response to one text.

Read the passage. Distribute pages 22–23 to students. Depending on students' needs, you may wish to read the passage aloud, have students read it with a partner, or have them read it independently.

Read and analyze the prompt. Read the prompt at the bottom of page 23 with students. Model how to analyze the prompt. Ask questions such as the following:

- *What form of writing does the prompt ask for?* (informative/ explanatory)

- *How can you tell?* (The prompt is asking me to explain something and provide information.)

- *What are the purposes of the assignment?* (to explain a topic and give information about it)

- *What information do I need to complete the task?* (I need to use evidence from the passage "The Great Pyramid of Giza.")

COMMON CORE
STATE STANDARD
W.4.2

Plan the writing. Draw the following graphic organizer on the board. You may also wish to distribute the matching graphic organizer located on page 122. Use the following think-alouds to model how to complete the graphic organizer. Ask for student input as you fill in the chart on the board.

- *The writing prompt asks me to explain why and how the ancient Egyptians build the Great Pyramid.*

- *Next the prompt asks me to support my explanation with evidence from the passage.*

- *I will record my evidence—or reasons and supporting details—in the chart.*

- *To finish my writing, I need a concluding statement or paragraph.*

Topic:
Why and How the Ancient Egyptians Built the Great Pyramid
Main Idea 1: Why They Built It
Supporting Details: 1. King Khufu ordered people to build his pyramid, or burial chamber. 2. The ancient Egyptians built pyramids so they could bury their kings and queens with everything they might need in the afterlife. 3. Khufu wanted his pyramid to be the biggest ever.
Main Idea 2: How They Built It
Supporting Details: 1. No one is sure how people so long ago managed to build it. 2. They may have pushed each large stone up a ramp. 3. It took about ten thousand people more than twenty years to build the Great Pyramid.

Read and analyze the model. Distribute the student writing model and checklist on pages 24–25 to students. Read them aloud. Discuss with students whether or not the writer was successful at accomplishing this task. Ask them to complete the checklist as you discuss the informative/explanatory text.

COMMON CORE
STATE STANDARD

W.4.2

Read the passage below.

The Great Pyramid of Giza

1.   The Seven Wonders of the World are ancient structures that most people consider to be the most amazing of all time. These structures were built thousands of years ago before people had construction equipment like bulldozers to push the earth and cranes to lift heavy blocks. Many people consider the Great Pyramid of Giza to be the most remarkable of the Seven Wonders. Why? It is the oldest wonder and the only one still standing today.

2.   The Great Pyramid was built in ancient Egypt around 2560 B.C.E. Other pyramids are near the Great Pyramid, but they are smaller. The Great Pyramid was about 480 feet (146 meters) tall when it was first built. Over time, sand and wind decreased its height. It was the tallest structure in the world for nearly 4,000 years.

3.   In ancient Egypt, kings and queens were buried in pyramids, which were enormous tombs. People thought their rulers could take their belongings with them into the afterlife, so they filled their kings' and queens' pyramids with everything they could possibly ever need. An Egyptian king named Khufu oversaw the construction of his own burial tomb, the Great Pyramid. He wanted it to be larger than any pyramid ever built.

4.   No one is quite sure exactly how people thousands of years ago managed to build such an enormous pyramid. They made the structure with about two million stones— and each weighed two to fifteen tons!

(continued)

COMMON CORE
STATE STANDARD
W.4.2

(continued)

5.   Some scholars believe that many people pushed the stones, one at a time, up ramps. It most likely took about ten thousand people more than twenty years to build the Great Pyramid.

6.   People tried to make the Great Pyramid as beautiful as possible. They covered the outside with polished white stones. However, many of these stones were damaged by earthquakes in the Middle Ages. Most were then taken away and used for other purposes. The pyramid has three burial chambers. The first is underground. A statue of Khufu was once in the second. The third is Khufu's burial chamber.

> **Facts About the Great Pyramid**
>
> - Scientists believe that the construction of the Great Pyramid was completed during Khufu's lifetime.
> - The base of the Great Pyramid covers 13 acres of land.
> - The Great Pyramid and those around it can be seen from 30 miles (48 kilometers) away.
> - People are not allowed to climb on the Great Pyramid, but they can go inside it.

7.   While the Great Pyramid has been worn down over time, it still stands proudly today. It has survived for thousands of years as a reminder of the ancient Egyptians and the effort they put into building it. Many people now care for the Great Pyramid to ensure that it will remain standing for years to come.

Read and analyze the prompt.

Informative/Explanatory Prompt

Explain why and how the ancient Egyptians built the Great Pyramid. Support your explanation with evidence from "The Great Pyramid of Giza."

Common Core
State Standard
W.4.2

Read and analyze the model.

Why and How the Ancient Egyptians Built the Great Pyramid

Paulo Sanchez

The ancient Egyptians built the Great Pyramid because King Khufu ordered them to. Khufu wanted to oversee the construction of his own burial tomb. The ancient Egyptians believed that people could take their belongings with them into the afterlife. They built large pyramids as burial tombs for their kings and queens. They wanted their rulers to have everything they could possibly need in the afterlife. The Great Pyramid is the largest of the pyramids because Khufu wanted his pyramid to be the biggest ever.

No one is sure how people so long ago managed to build such a gigantic structure. Scholars think the ancient Egyptians may have pulled the stones used to build the pyramid up ramps. These stones weighed two to fifteen tons each, so it took about ten thousand people more than twenty years to build the pyramid.

Common Core Writing to Texts Grade 4 • ©2014 Newmark Learning, LLC

COMMON CORE
STATE STANDARD
W.4.2

✔ Writing Checklist: Informative/Explanatory

❏ The writer started with a clear topic statement.

❏ The writer grouped related information in paragraphs.

❏ The writer developed his topic with facts, definitions, concrete details, quotations, or other information and examples from the text.

❏ The writer linked ideas and information effectively using words, phrases, and clauses.

❏ The writer used precise language and terminology to explain the topic.

❏ The writer wrote a conclusion related to the information he presented.

❏ The writer reviewed his writing for good grammar.

❏ The writer reviewed his writing for capitalization, punctuation, and spelling.

COMMON CORE
STATE STANDARD
W.4.2

Writing an Informative/ Explanatory Text

Mini-Lesson 4: Writing to Multiple Texts

COMMON CORE STATE STANDARD W.4.2

Write informative/explanatory texts to examine a topic and convey ideas and information clearly.

a. Introduce a topic clearly and group related information in paragraphs and sections; include formatting (e.g., headings), illustrations, and multimedia when useful to aiding comprehension.

b. Develop the topic with facts, definitions, concrete details, quotations, or other information and examples related to the topic.

c. Link ideas within categories of information using words and phrases (e.g., *another, for example, also, because*).

d. Use precise language and domain-specific vocabulary to inform about or explain the topic.

e. Provide a concluding statement or section related to the information or explanation presented.

Explain to students that they will often encounter writing prompts that instruct them to respond directly to more than one passage. For example, they might have to read two informational passages about the same topic or two fiction passages by the same author. Then take the following steps to guide students through the process of writing an informative/explanatory piece in response to multiple texts.

Read the passages. Distribute pages 28–31 to students. Depending on students' needs, you may wish to read the passages aloud, have students read them with a partner, or have students read the passages independently.

Read and analyze the prompt. Read the prompt at the bottom of page 31 with students. Model how to analyze the prompt. Ask questions such as the following:

- *What form of writing does the prompt ask for?* (informative/explanatory)

- *How can you tell?* (The prompt is asking me to explain something and provide information.)

- *What are the purposes of the assignment?* (to explain a topic and give information about it)

- *What information do I need to complete the task?* (I need to use evidence from the passage "The Mighty Oak Tree" and the passage "The Beautiful Birch Tree.")

COMMON CORE
STATE STANDARD
W.4.2

Plan the writing. Draw the following graphic organizer on the board. You may also wish to distribute the matching graphic organizer located on page 123. Use the following think-alouds to model how to complete the graphic organizer. Ask for student input as you fill in the chart on the board.

- *The writing prompt asks me to explain how oak trees and birch trees are alike and how they are different.*

- *Now I will think about the second part of the prompt. It asks me to find evidence from both passages to support my explanation.*

- *I will record my evidence—or reasons and supporting details—in the chart.*

- *To finish my writing, I need a concluding statement or paragraph.*

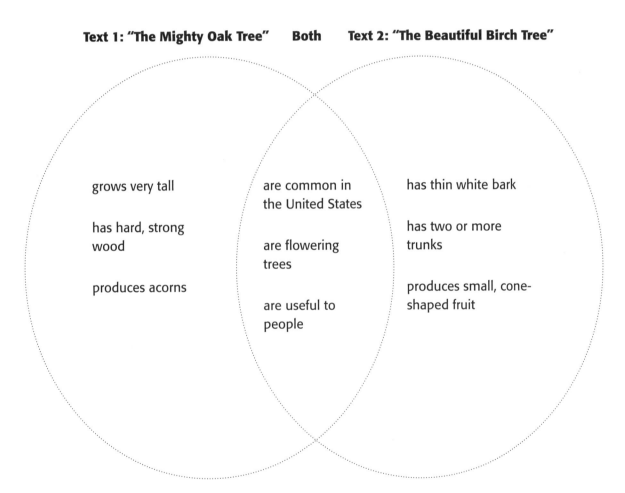

Text 1: "The Mighty Oak Tree"   Both   Text 2: "The Beautiful Birch Tree"

grows very tall

has hard, strong wood

produces acorns

are common in the United States

are flowering trees

are useful to people

has thin white bark

has two or more trunks

produces small, cone-shaped fruit

Read and analyze the model. Distribute the student writing model and checklist on pages 32–33 to students. Read them aloud. Discuss with students whether or not the writer was successful at accomplishing this task. Ask them to complete the checklist as you discuss the informative/explanatory text.

COMMON CORE
STATE STANDARD
W.4.2

Read the passages.

The Mighty Oak Tree

1.   Oak trees are among the most common trees in the United States. Many people also consider them some of the strongest trees because they grow very straight and tall. Oak wood is also hard and heavy, making it useful for many projects. Because of their strength and usefulness, oak trees are some of the most popular in the world.

2.   Hundreds of types of oak trees grow in the United States. These include the red oak, white oak, and live oak. Live oaks usually only grow to be about 50 feet (15 meters) tall. Red oaks are a middle-sized type of oak that can grow to be about 100 feet (30 meters) tall. White oaks are the tallest. They can reach a height of 130 feet (40 meters). That's taller than ten small houses stacked on top of one another!

3.   Different types of oak trees have different types of leaves. Some oak leaves have edges covered with small points. Others have smoother edges. In the fall, the leaves of most oak trees turn red, orange, or brown. After they change color, they fall off, and then new green leaves appear in the spring.

4.   Oaks are a type of flowering plant. This means that they produce flowers at certain times of the year. They also make a type of fruit called an acorn. Each acorn contains a seed that can grow into a new oak tree under the right conditions. Acorns grow on oak trees when the weather is warm. When cool fall weather arrives, acorns fall to the ground. Some of these acorns may begin growing into new trees even before the winter begins!

(continued)

Common Core
State Standard
W.4.2

(continued)

5. Oak trees have been useful to people for many years. Native Americans often used the bark and other parts of oak trees as medicine or for preparing animal hides. They also used acorns to make foods like acorn mush and acorn bread. Over time, people invented many other uses for oak trees. Europeans and others used strong and sturdy oak wood to build ships and buildings. People also learned that oak wood was good for burning. They could use it for campfires and cooking fires.

6. Oak trees still have many uses today. Oak wood is still widely used as lumber for building and flooring. It is also used to make things like furniture, barrels, and railroad ties. Oak trees play an important part in our everyday lives and continue to be a key natural material for people around the world.

(continue to next passage)

COMMON CORE
STATE STANDARD
W.4.2

(continued)

The Beautiful Birch Tree

1.   Birch trees are extremely common throughout the United States. Their thin white bark makes birches quite different from most other trees and plants. Many people consider birches to be some of the world's most beautiful trees. Birch trees also have many uses that make them important to people.

2.   Birch trees usually grow in places where the temperature and weather changes between seasons. They are most often found in Canada and the northeastern part of the United States. Birch trees usually do not live longer than 80 years.

3.   Birch trees can grow to be anywhere from 20 to 80 feet (6 to 24 meters) tall. The most common type of birch tree, the white or grey birch, usually grows to around 40 feet (12 meters) tall. The river birch can be up to 70 feet (21 meters) tall. Water birch is the smallest type of birch tree and only grows to around 20 feet (6 meters) tall. Still, that is about four times taller than the average person! Some birch trees grow in unusual ways. Many have two or more trunks that grow in different directions.

4.   Young birch trees start out with brown bark. As the tree gets older, its bark turns white. The outer bark of a birch tree is as thin as paper and can easily be peeled away from the trunk. The inner bark of most birch trees is usually a pinkish color. The bark at the base of a birch tree is often black! These surprising colors help give birches an interesting appearance.

5.   Birch leaves are usually small and either shaped like triangles or circles. They often have slightly pointy edges. Birch leaves turn yellow in the fall and drop to the ground before winter. New leaves begin to sprout in the springtime.

(continued)

Common Core Writing to Texts Grade 4 • ©2014 Newmark Learning, LLC

COMMON CORE
STATE STANDARD
W.4.2

(continued)

6.   Birch trees are flowering trees. They are also fruit-bearing trees that produce a small, cone-shaped fruit. This fruit is soft and can be easily broken apart. When the fruit falls and breaks apart, pieces can be moved by the wind and help grow new birch trees.

7.   People use birch trees for many purposes. Native Americans used birch bark to make canoes, bowls, and even walls for houses. Today, birch wood is often used to make furniture. It is also used to make a strong and cheap type of building material called plywood. In addition, the leaves of birch trees can be used to make certain kinds of tea and dye. Some people even use the sticky sap made by birch trees to make tasty syrup. Clearly, birch trees are both beautiful and useful.

Read and analyze the prompt.

Informative/Explanatory Prompt

Explain how oak trees and birch trees are alike and different. Use evidence from "The Mighty Oak Tree" and "The Beautiful Birch Tree" to support your explanation.

COMMON CORE
STATE STANDARD
W.4.2

Read and analyze the model.

Oak Trees and Birch Trees

by Alexandra Sanders

Oak trees and birch trees are alike in several ways. They are both common throughout the United States. They are both flowering trees that are useful to people. People use oak trees for lumber and to make things like furniture and railroad ties. People use birch trees to make things such as canoes and houses. Like oak trees, people use birch trees to make furniture.

Oak trees are different from birch trees because they are much taller and have only one trunk that grows straight up. One kind of oak tree can grow as tall as 130 feet (40 meters)!

Unlike oak trees, birch trees have thin, white bark. A birch tree can have two or more trunks that grow in different directions. Birch trees produce small, cone-shaped fruit, and not acorns like oak trees.

While oak trees and birch trees have some similarities, they are more different than they are alike.

COMMON CORE
STATE STANDARD
W.4.2

✔ Writing Checklist: Informative/Explanatory

❑ The writer started with a clear topic statement.

❑ The writer grouped related information in paragraphs.

❑ The writer developed her topic with facts, definitions, concrete details, quotations, or other information and examples from the text.

❑ The writer linked ideas and information effectively using words, phrases, and clauses.

❑ The writer used precise language and terminology to explain the topic.

❑ The writer wrote a conclusion related to the information she presented.

❑ The writer reviewed her writing for good grammar.

❑ The writer reviewed her writing for capitalization, punctuation, and spelling.

COMMON CORE
STATE STANDARD
W.4.3

Writing a Narrative

Mini-Lesson 5: Writing to One Text

> **COMMON CORE STATE STANDARD W.4.3**
>
> **Write narratives to develop real or imagined experiences or events using effective technique, descriptive details, and clear event sequences.**
>
> a. Orient the reader by establishing a situation and introducing a narrator and/or characters; organize an event sequence that unfolds naturally.
>
> b. Use dialogue and description to develop experiences and events or show the responses of characters to situations.
>
> c. Use a variety of transitional words and phrases to manage the sequence of events.
>
> d. Use concrete words and phrases and sensory details to convey experiences and events precisely.
>
> e. Provide a conclusion that follows from the narrated experiences or events.

Explain to students that they will often encounter narrative writing prompts that instruct them to respond directly to a text they have read. The text may be fiction or nonfiction. Then take the following steps to guide students through the process of writing a narrative piece in response to one text.

Read the passage. Distribute pages 36–37 to students. Depending on students' needs, you may wish to read the passage aloud, have students read it with a partner, or have them read it independently.

Read and analyze the prompt. Read the prompt at the bottom of page 37 with students. Model how to analyze the prompt. Ask questions such as the following:

- *What form of writing does the prompt ask for?* (narrative)

- *How can you tell?* (The prompt asks me to write a journal entry from Abeni's point of view about the day she and Mosi planted the carrot seeds.)

- *What is the purpose of the assignment?* (to write a journal entry)

- *What information do I need to complete the task?* (I need to use evidence from the story "Window Box.")

Plan the writing. Draw the following graphic organizer on the board. You may also wish to distribute the matching graphic organizer located on page 124. Use the following think-alouds to model how to complete the graphic organizer. Ask for student input as you fill in the chart on the board.

- *The writing prompt asks me to write a journal entry from Abeni's point of view about the day she and Mosi planted carrot seeds. I need to be sure that I tell what Abeni thinks and how she feels.*

- *I will record my events in the chart.*

- *To finish my writing, I need to include a new concluding statement for the journal entry.*

Sequence of Events

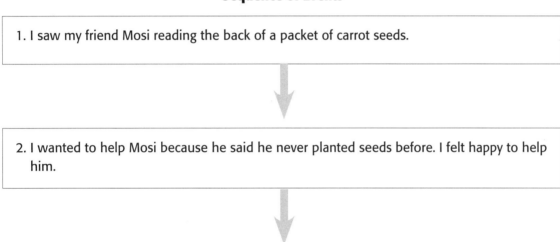

1. I saw my friend Mosi reading the back of a packet of carrot seeds.

2. I wanted to help Mosi because he said he never planted seeds before. I felt happy to help him.

3. I explained to him that he needed to plant the carrot seeds in potting soil and put them in full sun.

4. I borrowed a small shovel from my dad.

5. I shoveled soil in the pot and showed him where to plant the seeds. It was fun!

Read and analyze the model. Distribute the student writing model and checklist on pages 38–39 to students. Read them aloud. Discuss with students whether or not the writer was successful at accomplishing the task. Ask them to complete the checklist as you discuss the narrative.

Read the passage below.

Window Box

1. Ten-year-old Mosi sat on the front steps and pulled a packet of seeds out of his jacket. He turned over the little envelope, frowned, and began reading the information.

2. "Hello, Mosi. What are you doing?" asked his neighbor Abeni. She sat beside him and began reading the packet, too.

3. "Hi," Mosi replied. "My aunt gave me these carrot seeds. She said I could grow them in the window. She even left me some dirt and a flower pot, but I've never planted seeds before. She said to read the package and follow the directions."

4. Abeni grinned. "Actually, dirt for growing plants is called soil," she said. "Plants need the right kind of soil to be able to grow. Plants also need light and water to be healthy." She pointed to a picture of the sun on the packet. "These particular seeds need full sun to grow. Your windows get full sun."

5. Mosi thought of the many mornings he'd been awakened by blinding sunlight and nodded. "They should be planted one-eighth of an inch deep, which isn't very deep at all."

6. Abeni stood up. "My dad keeps a small shovel for repotting plants," she said. "I can borrow it and be back in two minutes." She leaped off the steps and skipped to her building before Mosi could answer and soon returned with a small shovel. "Dad says I can help you plant the carrots. Where's the soil?"

(continued)

(continued)

7. The pair climbed the stairs to Mosi's apartment. In the kitchen they discovered a bag containing potting soil and a long flower pot called a window box. Mosi carefully spread old newspapers over the counter. He opened the bag of soil and held it open while Abeni shoveled soil into the pot.

8. "That should be enough," she said, smoothing it with the shovel. Then she drew two long, shallow lines in the soil. "There's your farm field," she giggled.

9. Mosi tore open the packet and poured seeds into his palm. He dropped a pinch at a time the length of the rows, gently covered the seeds with one-eighth of an inch of soil, got water from the faucet, and soaked the soil.

10. Mosi put the pot in the window. He checked the soil every day and watered it when it became dry. On the twelfth day, he saw tiny green seedlings. With sun and water, they grew taller.

11. Thirty days later, Mosi knocked on Abeni's door with a delivery. "It's harvest time," he said, smiling, and presented her with a bunch of little carrots. "Thanks for helping me plant these."

12. Abeni grinned back. "You're welcome. The carrots are welcome, too—for dinner!"

Read and analyze the prompt.

Narrative Prompt

Write a journal entry from Abeni's point of view. Tell about the day she and Mosi planted carrot seeds. Make sure to tell what Abeni thinks and how she feels. Include details from the story "Window Box."

COMMON CORE
STATE STANDARD
W.4.3

Read and analyze the model.

Abeni's Journal Entry

by Joshua Latona

March 3

Today I saw my friend Mosi reading the back of a packet of carrot seeds that his aunt gave him. He wanted to grow them in a window box. He had never planted seeds before, so I knew I could help him. I love to plant seeds and grow things!

I explained to him that he needed to plant the carrot seeds in potting soil, not dirt. I told him that they need to grow in a place with full sun.

I went home to get the small shovel Dad uses to repot plants. When I returned, we found a bag of potting soil in Mosi's apartment. I helped him shovel the soil into the pot and drop seeds into rows in the dirt. Then he covered the seeds with one-eighth of an inch of soil and watered them. It was fun! I had a great day.

Common Core Writing to Texts Grade 4 • ©2014 Newmark Learning, LLC

✓ Writing Checklist: Narrative

❏   The writer established a setting or situation for his narrative.

❏   The writer introduced a narrator and/or characters.

❏   The writer organized his narrative into a sequence of unfolding events.

❏   The writer used dialogue and description to develop events and show how characters respond to them.

❏   The writer used transitional words to show the sequence of events.

❏   The writer used concrete words and phrases and sensory details to describe events.

❏   The writer wrote a conclusion to the events in his narrative.

❏   The writer reviewed his writing for good grammar.

❏   The writer reviewed his writing for capitalization, punctuation, and spelling.

COMMON CORE
STATE STANDARD
W.4.3

Writing a Narrative

Mini-Lesson 6: Writing to Multiple Texts

> **COMMON CORE STATE STANDARD W.4.3**
>
> **Write narratives to develop real or imagined experiences or events using effective technique, descriptive details, and clear event sequences.**
>
> a. Orient the reader by establishing a situation and introducing a narrator and/or characters; organize an event sequence that unfolds naturally.
>
> b. Use dialogue and description to develop experiences and events or show the responses of characters to situations.
>
> c. Use a variety of transitional words and phrases to manage the sequence of events.
>
> d. Use concrete words and phrases and sensory details to convey experiences and events precisely.
>
> e. Provide a conclusion that follows from the narrated experiences or events.

Explain to students that they will often encounter writing prompts that instruct them to respond directly to more than one passage. For example, they might have to read two fictional passages by the same author, two fictional passages with a similar theme, or two informational passages about the same topic. Then take the following steps to guide students through the process of writing a narrative piece in response to multiple texts.

Read the passages. Distribute pages 42–45 to students. Depending on students' needs, you may wish to read the passages aloud, have students read them with a partner, or have them read the passages independently.

Read and analyze the prompt. Read the prompt at the bottom of page 45 with students. Model how to analyze the prompt. Ask questions such as the following:

- *What form of writing does the prompt ask for?* (narrative)

- *How can you tell?* (The prompt asks me to write a sequel to the story.)

- *What are the purposes of the assignment?* (to write a story that shows the two main characters meeting)

- *What information do I need to complete the task?* (I need to use evidence from the story "No Longer the New Kid" and from the story "We're Moving Where?")

COMMON CORE
STATE STANDARD
W.4.3

Plan the writing. Draw the following graphic organizer on the board. You may also wish to distribute the matching graphic organizer located on page 125. Use the following think-alouds to model how to complete the graphic organizer. Ask for student input as you fill in the chart on the board.

- *The prompt asks me to imagine that Allison is a new kid at Jamie's school.*

- *The second part of the prompt asks me to write a sequel to "We're Moving Where?" in which Allison and Jamie meet, and he helps her solve a problem.*

- *I'll list the characters, setting, details from the text I read, events, problem, and resolution in the graphic organizer.*

Characters: Allison and Jamie	**Setting:** The next day at school
Goal/Problem/Conflict: Allison cannot find the classroom she needs to go to next.	

Details from Stories I Read: Allison is not happy because she had to leave her home and school in Florida and move to New York. Jamie has been in this situation. He moved from California to New York. At first, he was not a bit happy. However, now he likes New York and says it feels like home.	**New Events:** Jamie introduces himself to Allison in the hallway.
Ending/Resolution: Jamie walks Allison to class.	

Read and analyze the model. Distribute the student writing model and checklist on pages 46–47 to students. Read them aloud. Discuss with students whether or not the writer was successful at accomplishing this task. Ask them to complete the checklist as you discuss the narrative piece.

COMMON CORE
STATE STANDARD

W.4.3

Read the passages.

No Longer the New Kid

1.   Jamie was getting books out of his locker when his friend Manuel slapped him on the back. "Hey, buddy! Are we still going to play basketball after school today?" Manuel asked.

2.   "You bet," Jamie said. "Most of the guys in our class are going. Maybe afterward, we can go to my house for snacks."

3.   "Sounds like a plan," Manuel said and headed off to class.

4.   "Hi, Jamie," said Christina, one of Jamie's best friends. "Do you think you can help me with my English homework during study hall today? Last time you went over it with me, it really helped me understand it better."

5.   "Sure thing," Jamie said and thought about how much he liked his friends and this school. But he hadn't always felt this way.

6.   Jamie moved to New York from California two years ago. Both his mother and his father had lost their jobs, so Jamie and his family moved in temporarily with his grandparents. His parents decided to look for work in New York where his grandparents lived.

(continued)

(continued)

7.   Jamie was not pleased about having to leave sunny California, his friends, and his school to move to chilly New York. On his first day at his new school, he noticed how differently the New York kids dressed and talked. Jamie didn't want anything to do with them. He wanted to go home.

8.   For the first week, he tried very hard not to make friends. Sure, he responded politely to kids who spoke to him. But he promised himself that he would remain loyal to his friends and his old school. He didn't think it would take that long to convince his parents to go back to California and look for work there.

9.   He was unable to convince them, however. Jamie's mother was the first to find a job—and it was a good job, much better than the one she had lost in California. Within a month, his father also found a job, and they moved into their own place. Jamie realized that he was stuck in New York for good. After a while, Jamie felt lonely sitting by himself at lunch and trying hard to not talk to anyone. He finally let himself get to know some of his classmates. His initial impression about them was right—they were different for sure, but they were also very nice.

10.   Now, it seemed as if he'd always lived here. He had many good friends and was on the basketball team. He didn't even mind dressing for the cold winters because New York now felt like home.

(continue to next passage)

COMMON CORE
STATE STANDARD

W.4.3

(continued)

We're Moving Where?

1. Allison shivered when she stepped out the car. "Why didn't you wear a coat?" her mother asked.

2. "Because I don't like coats," Allison said. "If we were home, we wouldn't have to wear coats—or socks for that matter."

3. Allison's mother sighed. "Allison, we've been over this. We live in New York now, not Florida."

4. A month ago, Allison's mother told her and her little brother Lance that they were moving from Florida to New York. Allison's grandparents were getting older, and they needed family close by. Allison's grandfather ran a successful bakery. He wanted to retire, and he wanted his daughter—Allison's mother—to take over the family business. Allison knew her mother was excited about the opportunity, so Allison tried to be nice, but this was sometimes difficult because Allison felt as if her entire world had changed.

5. When Allison and her mother sat in the principal's office filling out paperwork, Allison worried that she might start to cry. The kids in the hallway looked so strange in their heavy sweaters and scarves. How would she ever adjust to living in this frozen tundra?

6. The principal seemed to sense her anxiety and excused herself and then left the room. When she returned, she was with a girl who looked about Allison's age. The girl had red hair and freckles and a warm smile.

7. "Allison," the principal said, "this is Olivia. She'll be in your homeroom and in most of your classes."

(continued)

(continued)

8. Olivia extended her hand and Allison shook it. "I'll show you around, okay? I'll introduce you to some nice kids." Allison took a deep breath and thanked Olivia. Then the two girls headed to class.

9. "So how was it?" her mother asked hopefully when Allison returned home after school. "Not terrible," Allison said. "The kids are really nice, but I still want to go home." Allison's mother put her arm around her daughter's shoulders and hugged her.

Read and analyze the prompt.

Narrative Prompt

Imagine that Allison is the new kid at Jamie's school. Write a sequel to "We're Moving Where?" in which Allison and Jamie meet, and he helps her solve a problem.

COMMON CORE
STATE STANDARD

W.4.3

Read and analyze the model.

Sequel to "We're Moving Where?"

by Michelle Winters

When Allison walked into her homeroom the next morning, she looked at her schedule. She had no idea where her first class was other than that it might be on the first floor. She didn't see Olivia, and felt uncomfortable asking anyone else. They were all chatting happily about things Allison knew nothing about.

When the bell rang, the class headed into the hallway. Allison decided to keep walking around until she found room 184B. She was aware that all eyes would probably be on her when she walked in late for class.

Just then she saw a boy smiling at her. He walked over said, "I'm Jamie. Are you lost?"

Allison showed him the schedule. "Ah, that's at the very end of the hall and then down a flight of stairs. How about I walk you there?"

"Thank you," Allison said and sighed.

"I know it feels terrible being new, but this is a really nice school and the people here are great once you get to know them," he explained. Then, as they walked, he told Allison about his move from California to New York.

By the time they arrived at her class, Allison felt as if she had made a friend. "Thanks so much, Jamie," she said with a smile.

✓ Writing Checklist: Narrative

❏ The writer established a setting or situation for her narrative.

❏ The writer introduced a narrator and/or characters.

❏ The writer organized her narrative into a sequence of unfolding events.

❏ The writer used dialogue and description to develop events and show how characters respond to them.

❏ The writer used transitional words to show her sequence of events.

❏ The writer used concrete words and phrases and sensory details to describe events.

❏ The writer wrote a conclusion to the events in her narrative.

❏ The writer reviewed her writing for good grammar.

❏ The writer reviewed her writing for capitalization, punctuation, and spelling.

Practice Texts with Prompts
How to Use Practice Texts with Prompts

This section of *Writing to Texts* provides opportunities for students to practice writing frequently in a wide range of genres and provides authentic practice for standardized writing assessments. Each practice lesson contains a passage or pair of passages followed by three prompts.

Before beginning, assign students one of the prompts, or ask them each to choose one. Explain to students that they are to plan and write an essay about the passage or passages according to the instructions in the chosen prompt. They should write on a separate piece of paper, or in a writing journal designated for writing practice.

There are various ways to use the practice section. You may wish to have students complete the writing tasks at independent workstations, as homework assignments, or as test practice in a timed environment.

If you choose to use these as practice for standardized tests, assign one prompt and give students 60 minutes to execute the task. In using these as test practice, tell students that they should think of their writing as a draft, and tell them they will not have additional time to revise their work.

You may also choose to have students respond to the prompts orally to strengthen academic oral language skills.

Graphic organizers for each type of writing are included on pages 120–125. You may choose to distribute them to help students plan and organize. On pages 126–127, reproducible Student Writing Checklists are provided. Distribute them to students to serve as checklists as they write, or as self-assessment guides.

Conducting Research

The Common Core State Standards require that students are provided opportunities to learn research techniques and to apply these skills in their preparation of projects. The passages in this section can make for research project starters. After students respond to an informational prompt, ask them to conduct further research on information from the practice text in order to build their knowledge.

Explain to students that researchers take good notes, connect new knowledge to what is already known, organize information into sensible layouts for a report, cite their sources, and use their own words to convey the information.

Tell students to gather information from print and digital sources. Have them take brief notes on sources and sort their facts, details, and evidence into categories. They may choose an appropriate organizer from pages 120–125.

Practice Texts and Prompts Table of Contents

COMMON CORE
STATE STANDARDS
W.4.1–
W.4.10

Name_____ Date_____

Read the passage below.

Dust Bowl—North Texas, 1934

1.   Emily Adams crept to the corner of the house. The paint here was almost gone, ripped off by the dust storms. She paused and listened for the gentle "cluck, cluck" of the chickens. Seven were already in the crate, but the eighth chicken was difficult to catch. Nine-year-old Emily leaned around the corner and saw the hen on the wheelbarrow. She stretched out her hand, but the bird suddenly jumped away. However, just as Emily was ready to give up, her brother jumped off the back step and scooped up the hen.

2.   "Come on, January, in the box with your sisters," five-year-old Teddy said as he carried the chicken to the front yard. Emily watched him walking, dust swelling around him as his bare feet sank into the ground. Mama and Papa were waiting.

3.   For three years Papa had planted crops that failed. The rain did not come, and the wind roared across the plains, taking away the rich soil. Families packed up and moved away.

4.   Emily followed slowly, first looking at the miles of bare prairie they were leaving behind, and then turning her head to glance at the house. The curtains were drawn. The windows had been closed for months, but the wind pushed the dust in around the edges. Now they were leaving the dust in Texas and going west, where Papa would start a new job.

(continued)

Name_____ Date_____

COMMON CORE
STATE STANDARDS
W.4.1–
W.4.10

(continued)

5.　　Mama helped Emily and Teddy into the truck as Papa put the chickens in the back with the furniture. They drove down the country road. Emily would miss her friends, but many of them had already moved away. "You'll make new friends," Mama said. Bravely Emily smiled. She would finally meet her cousins in California, Mama said. The whole family would be together.

6.　　Papa turned the truck onto the main road. Soon Teddy was asleep. He hugged his little truck, the one Papa had made from some extra wood. He leaned against Emily, so she carefully moved her doll, Abigail, so she wouldn't be flattened.

7.　　Emily closed her eyes, and when she opened them, Mama was looking at her through the window. "Are you hungry?" she asked, holding up a sandwich wrapped in a tea towel. Emily stretched and opened the door. She stood beside the truck eating her sandwich while Teddy rubbed his eyes and yawned, and then took a big bite of his lunch.

8.　　The Adamses drove for days to reach California. At night, they found quiet spots for Papa to park the truck and slept on the ground. Sometimes a friendly farmer would let them sleep in his barn. Every day, the world was less dusty.

COMMON CORE
STATE STANDARDS
W.4.1–
W.4.10

Name_____ Date_____

Opinion/Argument Prompt

Do you think the Adams family make a good choice in deciding to move? Why or why not? Support your opinion with reasons from the text.

Informative/Explanatory Prompt

What can you tell about Mama from the story? What kind of person is she? Use specific details from the text to support your explanation.

Narrative Prompt

Write a journal entry Emily might have recorded the day she and her family left their home in Texas.

Name_____ Date_____

COMMON CORE
STATE STANDARDS
W.4.1–
W.4.10

Read the passage below.

Front-Page News

1. *Setting: A classroom with desks, chairs, and several computers.*

2. *(Children enter from the left and gather around a computer. Nine-year-old Gavin and ten-year-old Martina look at the screen before walking to the front of the stage.)*

3. **Gavin:** The *Westfield Weekly* goes to press tomorrow, and we still don't have a front-page story. *(He grips his forehead.)* Why does this always happen?

4. **Martina:** Why do you always worry? Have I ever let you down? *(pulls a camera from her pocket and waves it in front of him)* I will have a great picture and a complete front-page story by the time the bell rings for lunch.

5. **Gavin:** No, please. I've already seen photos of your goldfish. He is not smiling; that's just his face.

6. **Martina:** Yes he is! *(stops and shakes her head, sighing)* Okay, no goldfish. I will be talking to someone soon. *(looks at her watch)* Now, actually.

7. *(A boy enters and walks up to Martina and Gavin. He is carrying a box.)*

8. **Lucas:** Hi, Martina.

9. **Martina:** Hi! Just let me get a pen and paper, and you can tell me all about your project. *(turns away to get a notebook from a desk)*

10. **Gavin:** *(to Martina)* Project? You're writing about someone's homework?

(continued)

COMMON CORE
STATE STANDARDS
W.4.1–
W.4.10

Name_____ Date_____

(continued)

11. **Martina:** Not that kind of project. Lucas has a hobby. He's going to tell me everything about it, and I'm going to write a story for the newspaper.

12. **Gavin:** What kind of hobby? *(to Lucas)* Do you collect baseball cards or something?

13. **Lucas:** No, but I like baseball. My hobby is knitting.

14. **Gavin:** Knitting? As in knitting sweaters?

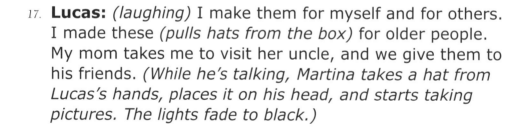

15. **Lucas:** *(shrugging)* Mostly I make scarves and hats. People think it's difficult, but it really isn't. It's fun to make things.

16. **Martina:** *(already writing in her notebook)* Do you make them for yourself or for other people?

17. **Lucas:** *(laughing)* I make them for myself and for others. I made these *(pulls hats from the box)* for older people. My mom takes me to visit her uncle, and we give them to his friends. *(While he's talking, Martina takes a hat from Lucas's hands, places it on his head, and starts taking pictures. The lights fade to black.)*

18. *(When the lights come on, Lucas and Martina are sitting at a desk knitting while other students look over their shoulders. Gavin is standing nearby, examining the school newspaper and nodding.)*

19. **Gavin:** Your photos are great, Martina! You did a nice job on this front-page story.

20. **Martina:** And Lucas did a great job with those hats. So many people want to make them that he's starting a knitting club. In fact *(reaches for her notebook)*, that could be the next front-page story!

Name_____ Date_____

COMMON CORE
STATE STANDARDS
W.4.1–
W.4.10

Opinion/Argument Prompt

Do you think an article about Lucas's hobby is a good front-page story for a school newspaper? Why or why not? Support your opinion with details from the play.

Informative/Explanatory Prompt

Explain how Gavin and Martina are alike and different. Use evidence from the play to support your ideas. Be sure to point out what each character says and does.

Narrative Prompt

Write a story about what happens when the knitting club has its first meeting. Use details and characters from the play. Make sure your story has a beginning, middle, and end, and includes descriptions and dialogue.

Common Core
State Standards
W.4.1–
W.4.10

Name_____ Date_____

Read the passage below.

Amaterasu the Sun Goddess

A Japanese Myth

1. Amaterasu, the Japanese goddess of the sun, helped rule the universe. She shared power with her two brothers. People worshipped Amaterasu because she provided light, which made the rice grow. They loved her beauty, warmth, and concern for those who needed help.

2. Trouble started when Amaterasu's brother Susano'o, the storm god, had to make a trip to the underworld. He was supposed to rescue a good spirit, but he was afraid of the bad spirits that also lived there. He decided to visit his sister in the hope that she could comfort him.

3. However, he was so scared and so eager to see her that when he flew across the sky, he created so much lightning and thunder that he frightened everyone on Earth. His stormy arrival even scared Amaterasu.

4. Susano'o visited for days until a disagreement with his sister threw him into a rage. His hurricane of anger destroyed the rice fields and filled Amaterasu's temples with mud.

5. Amaterasu was angry with her brother, but out of pity she offered him some of her own strength to help him get into and out of the underworld. But this only made the disagreement worse.

6. Susano'o felt his sister didn't understand him and thought she was stronger than he was. He sent more terrors to Amaterasu's palace.

(continued)

Name_____ Date_____

(continued)

7.   Amaterasu was so upset that she ran away and hid in a cave and sealed it shut with a boulder. This was not good for Earth. Without the sun goddess, there was no light or warmth in the world. The crops began to shrivel and die. People were cold and hungry and lost all hope.

8.   Susano'o left for the underworld in disgrace. The other gods made a plan to get Amaterasu out of the cave. They placed a mirror near the entrance of the cave and then made a great noise, laughing and cheering. Curious, Amaterasu peeked out and asked what was going on. One of the gods told her that there was a new goddess—and then he pointed to the mirror.

9.   Amaterasu was surprised to see another goddess that was as bright as she was. She slipped out of the cave to get a closer look. The gods quickly closed the cave with the rock so she couldn't get back in. Then they pleaded with her to return to the sky and shine so crops would grow again. Seeing herself had given her strength, and she returned to her palace and her duties.

10.   Amaterasu promised that she would never leave the heavens again, and the people of Japan lived on with renewed courage and joy.

Common Core
State Standards

W.4.1–
W.4.10

Name_____ Date_____

Opinion/Argument Prompt

According to the myth, people love Amaterasu. How do you think they feel about Susano'o? Support your opinion with evidence from the text.

Informative/Explanatory Prompt

How do the gods get Amaterasu to come out of the cave? Support your explanation with details from the text.

Narrative Prompt

Write an apology letter from Susano'o to Amaterasu. As Susano'o, explain your actions and tell how you have changed. Try to convince Amaterasu to forgive you.

Name_____ Date_____

COMMON CORE
STATE STANDARDS
W.4.1–
W.4.10

Read the passage below.

Welcome, Nana!

1.　Alda awoke early and for a minute couldn't remember why the day was different. Oh, yes—Nana was visiting! Alda and her brother, Max, wanted to make Nana's first morning with them very special.

2.　First, though, Alda put on her slippers and crept quietly into the hall. Looking down the stairs, she could see Nana's coat on the hook. Dad had brought Nana to their house very late—Alda and Max had fallen asleep waiting. Alda quickly opened the door to Max's room and slipped inside.

3.　"Max," she whispered into his ear, "wake up! Nana's here!" Max's eyes popped wide open.

4.　"Did I oversleep?" he asked, alarmed that their plans were ruined.

5.　"No, I just woke up," Alda replied. She helped her little brother find his slippers, and then led him downstairs to the kitchen. Dad had helped them prepare the surprise yesterday before he left for the airport. Two trays waited on the table.

6.　Max carefully placed spoons and napkins on each tray, and then took two plates and two bowls from the cupboard. Alda placed two small glasses on the counter. She took orange juice out of the refrigerator and filled the glasses.

7.　Alda put the juice bottle away and took whole-wheat muffins, fruit, and yogurt from the refrigerator. As Max put a muffin on each plate, Alda spooned yogurt into the bowls. She handed a spoon to Max. She watched as he counted out strawberries and grapes, putting the same number in each bowl of yogurt.

(continued)

COMMON CORE
STATE STANDARDS
W.4.1–
W.4.10

Name_____ Date_____

(continued)

8. "Wait!" said Max as Alda picked up a tray. She raised an eyebrow. Max grinned and pointed to the window. Alda smiled, too. She put the tray down and reached up to the windowsill. Max took the daisies and put them next to the juice glasses. Together Max and Alda carried the trays upstairs.

9. Dad was standing in the hall, yawning. He smiled as Max and Alda crept past the baby's room. "You were so quiet that I thought you were still asleep," he whispered. The door behind him opened, and Mama looked out.

10. "What's this?" she asked, looking at Max, Alda, and the breakfast trays. Then Mama smiled and stepped out of her room. She understood the surprise was for her too. She softly knocked on Nana's door and went in.

11. "Hi, Mom!" she said. Mama sat on the bed and kissed her mother, while Nana hugged her tightly. As Max and Alda gave each of them a tray, they heard a baby cry.

12. "Oh, I can't wait to meet my new grandson!" Nana cried. Dad left the room and returned with Peter. The baby stopped wiggling and stared at everyone. "Good morning, Peter!" said Nana. "You're just in time for breakfast."

Name_____ Date_____

COMMON CORE
STATE STANDARDS
W.4.1–
W.4.10

Opinion/Argument Prompt

How do you think Alda and Max feel about Nana? Support your opinion with details from the text.

Informative/Explanatory Prompt

Create a checklist that Alda and Max could use when they are preparing breakfast for Nana and Mama. Then write a paragraph explaining why each item on the list is necessary. Use details from the text.

Narrative Prompt

Write a story about what happens while Nana, Alda, and Max are eating breakfast. Include descriptions and dialogue. Use details from the story "Welcome, Nana!"

COMMON CORE
STATE STANDARDS
W.4.1–
W.4.10

Name_____ Date_____

Read the passage below.

The Tale of Arachne

1.　Athena, the goddess of wisdom, was one of the most beloved of the Greek gods. She was known as a great weaver and enjoyed teaching her followers about her art. Athena was always proud of her students and their work as long as they were thankful for her help.

2.　Arachne was a poor young girl who learned to weave from Athena. She became so good at weaving that her work was just as good as her teacher's. People came from far and wide to see her creations. Some even came just to watch her work!

3.　The people who traveled to see Arachne were so amazed that many of them asked her if she had learned her skills from Athena. However, Arachne was so full of pride that she didn't want to admit that Athena had taught her. She told everyone that she developed her skills on her own without any help from the goddess. She even claimed that she was better at weaving than Athena herself.

4.　Athena was deeply hurt when she heard Arachne's claims and decided to pay her old student a visit. She changed herself to look like an old woman and went to Arachne's house to give her a chance to apologize for what she had said.

5.　Athena confronted Arachne in disguise and warned her that it was a bad idea to test the gods. Arachne ignored the warning and yelled back at the old woman, "If Athena doesn't like what I have to say, let her come here and challenge me!"

6.　Athena was angered by Arachne's response. She immediately returned to her normal form and revealed herself to Arachne. Arachne had no choice but to stay true to her word and agree to a weaving contest with Athena.

(continued)

Common Core Writing to Texts Grade 4 • ©2014 Newmark Learning, LLC

Name_____ Date_____

COMMON CORE
STATE STANDARDS
W.4.1–
W.4.10

(continued)

7.   Soon the pair sat down and began to weave. Athena wove as fast as she could and created a beautiful design. Arachne wove a design that some thought was even more beautiful than Athena's.

8.   Athena looked at Arachne's finished work at the end of the contest and thought it was an insult to the gods. She asked Arachne to apologize, but the young woman refused. Athena then destroyed Arachne's loom in a fit of anger. This caused Arachne to suddenly feel guilty for all she had said and done.

9.   Athena scolded Arachne. "Since you are so proud of your work, I'll see that you keep weaving forever!" Arachne's head began to shrink and her fingers turned into long legs. Athena turned her into a spider and left her to spin webs for the rest of her life.

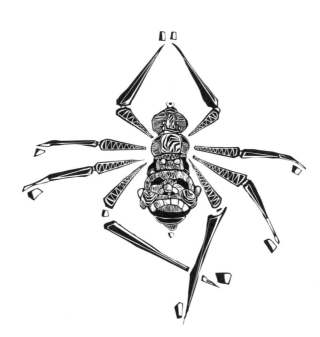

COMMON CORE
STATE STANDARDS
W.4.1–
W.4.10

Name_____ Date_____

Opinion/Argument Prompt

Do you think Athena treats Arachne fairly? Why or why not? Support your opinion with reasons from the text.

Informative/Explanatory Prompt

What lesson does Athena teach Arachne? State the lesson and explain how Athena teaches it. Use specific details and words from the story to support your explanation.

Narrative Prompt

Retell the story from Arachne's point of view. Be sure to include Arachne's thoughts and feelings about what happens. Use details from the "The Tale of Arachne" in your new story.

Name_____ Date_____

COMMON CORE
STATE STANDARDS
W.4.1–
W.4.10

Read the passage below.

What's That Smell?

1.   The nose catches a wonderful scent coming from the kitchen in the morning. It smells like waffles and maple syrup. What a yummy way to start the day. In the kitchen, the eyes and nose agree. A plate of waffles and syrup sits on the table. How clever the nose is! How is it able to notice scents in the air? How can it tell the difference between a homemade breakfast and a dirty sock?

2.   Everything with a smell has scent molecules. Molecules are tiny pieces of something. Molecules are so small that they can't be seen without a microscope. A ripe tomato, a blade of cut grass, and an apple pie all give off scent molecules. How do scent molecules get into the air? Scent molecules are very light—so light they float into the air. When a person takes a breath of air, the scent molecules enter his or her nose right along with the air.

3.   Air enters the nose through openings called nostrils. Air moves through the nose to an opening behind it. There, the air hits an area about the size of a postage stamp. This area is full of special cells that can sense smells. The cells are called neurons. There are millions of neurons in this area. The neurons are covered with tiny hairs. Inside these hairs are even smaller receptors. These receptors contain pockets that trap scent molecules from the air.

4.   When a receptor catches a scent molecule, the receptor changes shape. This causes the neuron to send a message to the brain. From this message, the brain can tell exactly what scent the nose can smell. The most amazing part is that all this happens in a split second!

(continued)

Common Core
State Standards
W.4.1–
W.4.10

Name_____ Date_____

(continued)

5.   Scientists have studied humans' sense of smell for a long time. They learned that each receptor can sense only certain scent molecules. But a smell may not contain just one type of scent molecule. For example, perfume can contain many different scent molecules. When a person smells perfume, his or her receptors catch different scent molecules from the air.

6.   The receptors then send messages to the brain. The brain thinks about the messages it receives and uses them to figure out what smell the nose has noticed. Scientists think that the brain can tell the difference among 10,000 different smells!

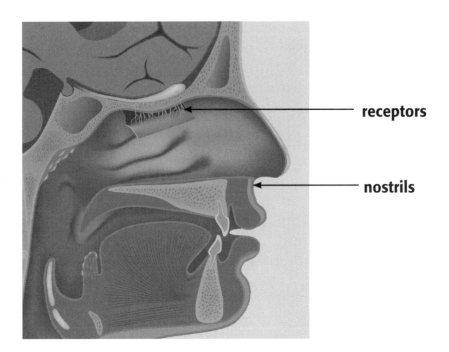

receptors

nostrils

Name_____ Date_____

Common Core
State Standards
W.4.1–
W.4.10

Opinion/Argument Prompt

**How do you think the author feels about the sense of smell?
Support your opinion with details from the text.**

Informative/Explanatory Prompt

**Explain to a friend how her sense of smell helps her tell the
difference between a homemade breakfast and a dirty sock.
Use specific details from the text in your explanation.**

Narrative Prompt

**Write a story from the point of view of a scent molecule.
Identify what kind of scent you are, where you came from,
and how you register in someone's brain. Use details from the
text in your story.**

COMMON CORE
STATE STANDARDS
W.4.1–
W.4.10

Name_____ Date_____

Read the passage below.

Katherine Sui Fun Cheung

1.   Katherine Sui Fun Cheung was born in China in 1904. At this time, most women were wives and mothers. Girls did not grow up to have adventures—but Katherine became the first Chinese American woman pilot in the United States.

2.   Katherine moved to the United States in 1921 when she was seventeen. She studied music at the University of Southern California in Los Angeles. One day, Katherine's father took her to an airfield to teach her to drive a car. Katherine liked driving, but she liked watching planes take off and land even more. She wanted to learn to fly but had to wait another ten years to do this.

3.   Katherine soon decided to get married. She kept her own last name, which was something else girls did not do back then. She had two daughters with her husband, George Young. Then in 1932 her cousin invited Katherine to fly in a plane. Katherine loved flying. She took lessons with the Chinese Aeronautical Association and quickly earned her pilot's license. She was the first Chinese American woman licensed to fly a plane in the United States. She was one of only about 200 women in the country to have a pilot's license.

4.   Though Katherine enjoyed flying, she loved acrobatics the most. She flew loops and barrel rolls, and learned to fly upside down. She performed at fairs and competed in races.

5.   In 1935 the world's most famous female pilot, Amelia Earhart, invited Katherine to join a club. The Ninety-Nines were female pilots who encouraged women to learn to fly. After she joined the club, Katherine raced other famous pilots. She was not afraid to match her old plane against newer planes. She also studied and earned a license to fly larger planes.

(continued)

Name_____ Date_____

(continued)

6.   Katherine often traveled to speak to Chinese American groups. She wanted other Chinese women to learn to fly. When Japan invaded China in 1937, many Chinese Americans wanted to defend China. Katherine wanted to fly to China and teach women to fly so they could join the Chinese Air Force. She also wanted to deliver medical supplies to China. She stopped competing in air races and performing stunts. Instead she went to China and opened a flight school. She stayed there for five years.

7.   Katherine's father worried about his daughter's daring adventures. He made her promise she would not fly again, and Katherine felt bad because her friend, Amelia Earhart, had disappeared while attempting to fly around the world. When she was thirty-eight years old, Katherine stopped flying. However, even after retiring her "wings," Katherine continued to inspire other women to follow their dreams.

COMMON CORE
STATE STANDARDS
W.4.1–
W.4.10

Name_____ Date_____

Opinion/Argument Prompt

Do you think Katherine Sui Fun Cheung was a role model?
Why or why not? Support your opinion with reasons
from the text.

Informative/Explanatory Prompt

In paragraph 7 the author states, "Katherine continued to
inspire other women to follow their dreams." Explain why
Katherine Sui Fun Cheung was and is an inspiration to others.
Include facts and details from the text in your explanation.

Narrative Prompt

Write a story about the Ninety-Nines. Use details from the
text to help you. Make sure you include characters, a setting,
descriptions, and dialogue in your story.

Name_____ Date_____

Read the passage below.

How to Make a Rainbow

1.   When a rainy day suddenly turns sunny, a colorful rainbow may appear in the sky and brighten everyone's spirits. Since rainbows only appear when the weather is just right, however, they can't be seen very often. Luckily it's possible to make an indoor rainbow that can be seen at any time!

2.   There are several ways to make an indoor rainbow, but the best methods involve using water and light. These two methods are called the water-glass method and the flashlight method.

3.   The water-glass method must be done on a day when the sun is out. To begin, find a clear water glass, a bucket, a towel, a small table, and a sheet of paper. Once these supplies have been gathered, it's time to start making rainbows!

4.   First find a window that the sun is shining through. Make sure that both the inside and outside of the window can be easily reached. Next put a small table in front of the inside of the window, fill the glass with water, and place the glass on the table.

5.   Once that's done, put a sheet of paper down on the floor in front of the table. The paper can be any light color, but white works best. Now it's time to head outside. Fill up a bucket with hot water and carefully use a towel to wet the outside of the window. Finally head back inside and simply adjust the paper. When the sunlight shining through the window and the water glass hits the paper just right, a rainbow will appear!

(continued)

COMMON CORE
STATE STANDARDS
W.4.1–
W.4.10

Name_____ Date_____

(continued)

6. To make a rainbow on a cloudy day or at night, use the flashlight method. To do so, find a water glass, a flashlight, a piece of paper, scissors, and some tape. First fold the paper in half and carefully use a pair of scissors to cut a little triangle out of its middle.

7. Next unfold the paper. Tape the paper to the flashlight so the light will shine through the hole. Once the flashlight is ready, fill the glass with water.

8. Finally turn on the flashlight and point it straight down at the top of the water glass. As soon as the flashlight lights up the water, a rainbow will appear.

Name_____ Date_____

COMMON CORE
STATE STANDARDS
W.4.1–
W.4.10

Opinion/Argument Prompt

Imagine that you are going to make an indoor rainbow. Would you rather use the water-glass method or the flashlight method? Support your opinion with reasons from the text.

Informative/Explanatory Prompt

Compare and contrast the water-glass method and the flashlight method. Explain how they are alike and different using details from the text.

Narrative Prompt

Write a story in which a character makes an indoor rainbow. Be sure to tell how the character makes the rainbow and how he or she feels when it appears. Include details from the text.

COMMON CORE
STATE STANDARDS
W.4.1–
W.4.10

Name_____ Date_____

Read the passage below.

Climate—

1. refers to the weather in a region, or a place, over a long period of time. Regions with the same climate generally have the same weather.

Climate classifications—

1. Tropical

2. Tropical climates are found near the equator. They may be either tropical wet or tropical wet and dry. Regions with a **tropical wet climate** have only one season and the temperature stays about 80 degrees throughout the year. Rain is frequent. *Examples*: parts of Brazil and the Philippines.

3. Regions with a **tropical wet and dry climate** are also very warm but experience two seasons: a wet season and a dry season. *Examples:* parts of Africa and India.

2. Moderate

4. Regions with a moderate climate have mild weather. There are three types of moderate climates: Mediterranean, humid subtropical, and marine west coast. Areas with a **Mediterranean climate** have a mild summer and a cool, wet winter. The temperature ranges from 30 to 60 degrees Fahrenheit (1 to 16 degrees Celsius) in winter and 50 to 72 degrees Fahrenheit (10 to 22 degrees Celsius) in summer. *Examples:* parts of California and Europe.

5. Regions with a **humid subtropical climate** experience hot summers and mild winters. Rain falls throughout the year. The high temperatures in these places quickly evaporate rainwater, making the weather very humid. *Example:* Florida.

6. Regions with a **marine west coast climate** have both summer and winter but the temperature is fairly mild during both seasons. The temperature ranges from about 30 degrees Fahrenheit (1 degree Celsius) in winter to 70 degrees Fahrenheit (21 degrees Celsius) in summer. Areas with this type of climate are near the ocean, which makes them cool and wet. *Example:* much of Europe.

(continued)

Name_____ Date_____

COMMON CORE
STATE STANDARDS
W.4.1–
W.4.10

(continued)

3. Continental

7. There are two types of continental climates: humid continental and subarctic. Regions with a **humid continental climate** have four seasons. Summer is warm and humid, fall is cool and dry, winter is very cold, and spring is warm and wet. *Example:* the northeastern United States.

8. Regions with a **subarctic climate** have two seasons: winter and summer. Winter is much longer than summer and very cold. Summer is also cool and lasts only from one to three months. Subarctic regions are covered in snow throughout most of the year. *Examples:* eastern Oregon and Idaho.

4. Polar

9. A polar climate may be either tundra or ice cap. Areas with a **tundra climate** have harsh winters and cool summers. During the winter, the temperature might drop to −50 degrees Fahrenheit (−46 degrees Celsius). These areas receive only a low level of precipitation. *Examples:* Greenland and parts of Alaska.

10. Only regions near the North and South Poles have an **ice cap climate**. Temperatures may never rise above freezing. *Examples:* North and South Poles.

5. Dry

11. A dry climate may be arid or semi-arid. Deserts, which are always dry, have an **arid climate**.

12. Regions with a **semi-arid climate** are between arid regions and wetter places. These regions are very dry but some are extremely cold. They frequently experience droughts. *Example:* parts of the Great Plains.

COMMON CORE
STATE STANDARDS

W.4.1–
W.4.10

Name_____ Date_____

Opinion/Argument Prompt

Which climate do you think would make for the best place to live? Support your opinion with details from the text.

Informative/Explanatory Prompt

Explain how a humid continental climate is different from a subarctic climate. Use details from the text to support your explanation.

Narrative Prompt

Imagine you are someone who lives in an area with a tundra climate. Write a story about what you did one day during the winter. Use details from the text as well as your own ideas.

Common Core Writing to Texts Grade 4 • ©2014 Newmark Learning, LLC

Name_____ Date_____

COMMON CORE
STATE STANDARDS
W.4.1–
W.4.10

Read the passage below.

Meeting Kimberly

1.   I'll never forget the day I met my best friend Kimberly. Kimberly and her family were moving into the house down the street. No one around knew anything about them other than that they just moved here from a big city and were therefore likely very snobby.

2.   I caught a glimpse of Kimberly early that day. I was riding my bike on the street and saw the moving van in front of the house. I pretended that I didn't see Kimberly—but I saw her! She looked gorgeous. She wore her shiny blonde hair in a ponytail and was dressed in a pale yellow shirt-and-short set that perfectly matched the color of her hair. She wore bangle bracelets on her wrists and bright white sandals. *No thank you*, I remember thinking. She and I obviously had nothing in common.

3.   My mother, however, thought otherwise. "I met the Petersons this morning, the new family moving in on our street," she explained. "They have a daughter named Kimberly who is your age. I told them that you'd stop by today and introduce yourself. Maybe you could ask her to go roller-skating with you and your friends tonight?"

4.   "Mom!" I exclaimed. "How could you do that? Did you see her? She's a city girl. We're not going to have anything in common. She's probably never been to a roller-skating rink in her life."

5.   "She seemed very nice to me, Lisa. And her mother said she is nervous about making new friends."

6.   I rolled my eyes and then thought that I might as well get this over with. Kimberly was sitting on her front porch when I rode my bike into her driveway. She waved and then stood. "I'm Kimberly," she said. "Are you Lisa? Your mom said you would stop by. She's really nice."

(continued)

COMMON CORE
STATE STANDARDS
W.4.1–
W.4.10

Name_____ Date_____

(continued)

7.   I nodded and introduced myself as Lisa Reynolds. I saw a novel on the table next to where Kimberly was sitting. It was not just any novel—it was a novel by Harriet Ellis, my favorite author. Kimberly and I chatted about the book. It turned out that she was also a huge Harriet Ellis fan. I discovered that my mother was right. Kimberly was really nice. We hit it off right away.

8.   "Hey, Kimberly," I said before I left, "do you like to roller-skate? My friends and I are going roller-skating tonight."

9.   "Are you kidding?" she asked. "I love roller-skating. I even have my own skates."

10.   "Great. We'll pick you up around six," I said.

11.   Somehow I knew after just one conversation that Kimberly and I would be friends for a very long time.

Name_____ Date_____

COMMON CORE
STATE STANDARDS
W.4.1–
W.4.10

Opinion/Argument Prompt

Do you think Lisa is being unfair at the beginning of the story? Why or why not? Support your opinion with details from the text.

Informative/Explanatory Prompt

Explain why Lisa does not want to meet Kimberly at first. Use details from the text to support your explanation.

Narrative Prompt

Retell the story from Kimberly's point of view. Include Kimberly's thoughts and feelings about Lisa. Have her describe what Lisa looks and acts like. Use details from "Meeting Kimberly" to help you.

COMMON CORE
STATE STANDARDS
W.4.1–
W.4.10

Name_____ Date_____

Read the passages.

From *Daniel and the Big Sky*

Missoula, Montana, 1984

Chapter 1

1. The sky suddenly darkened. Then the wind picked up. When a gust blew open the stable door, Dad ran out to close it. Then the pouring rain turned to hail and pelted the roof of the house. Large puddles covered what was once Daniel's family's yard.

2. Daniel and his family had lived in Montana for only a few months, and he had never seen a storm like this before. Then Daniel heard a loud crack, and the house went dark. A bolt of lightning had hit the telephone pole in front of the house. It had broken the pole, and wires now lay on the ground. Daniel picked up the phone, but the line was dead. He was glad his mother and Katherine were not there to witness this. They had driven to California to spend a week with Daniel's grandparents.

3. "Dad!" Daniel shouted. He could see his father leaning into the stables on a ladder. The wind had apparently broken one of the doors. Daniel knew that the horses must be frightened. He worried most about Mandy, their oldest horse. Her health had begun to decline, and she had become more nervous than usual.

4. Then just as quickly as it arrived, the storm ended. The dark clouds disappeared and daylight returned. The rain stopped and the wind died down.

5. Daniel headed outdoors to find his father. When he saw the ladder on the ground and his father lying next to it, he ran toward him. "Dad!" he shouted. "Are you okay?" But Daniel soon saw that his father was definitely not okay. His leg was bent at an odd angle, and he had a gash on his forehead. Daniel grabbed a towel and pushed it down hard over the gash.

(continued)

Name_____ Date_____

COMMON CORE
STATE STANDARDS
**W.4.1–
W.4.10**

(continued)

6.   "Can you get up?" he asked. "We need to get you some help." His father shook his head and said, "My leg is broken and I think some ribs are, too. Daniel, you're going to have to go into town and get some help."

7.   Daniel looked at the pickup truck parked near the house. "Dad, I have no idea how to drive yet."

8.   "You're going to have to ride one of the horses. Just ride straight along the road into town. There's a hospital right at the entrance. It won't take you more than a half-hour."

9.   Daniel nodded. There was only one problem. Daniel had not ridden a horse in two years, since he was twelve. He was riding Midnight, a friend's horse, when the horse became spooked and tossed Daniel off him like a rag doll. Daniel had broken his arm and swore he would never mount a horse again. Now he had no choice. He had to get to the hospital so they could send an ambulance for his father.

(continue to next passage)

COMMON CORE
STATE STANDARDS

W.4.1–
W.4.10

Name_____ Date_____

(continued)

Chapter 2

1. *You have nothing to fear but fear itself.* Daniel remembered his mother's words and tried to be brave. "Sadie, my lady, we can do this, right?" He spoke to the horse calmly, the way Katherine always had, even though his hands were trembling and he felt like he might cry. He gently rubbed Sadie's muzzle. Then he put his left foot in the stirrup and swung his right leg over Sadie's back. He tried to calm himself and push away the memory of the last time he had ridden a horse. "That's not going to happen this time," he said to himself.

2. Daniel had chosen to ride Sadie even though Riot was larger and faster. Riot could be unpredictable, though, and Daniel did not want to take a chance on getting thrown again. If that happened, what would happen to his dad? Sadie was Katherine's horse and a gentle soul. She let his ten-year-old sister ride her daily without incident. Daniel trusted Sadie. She would get him to the hospital safely.

3. Daniel guided Sadie out of the stables. The horse's first instinct was to turn left toward the trails, but Daniel guided her to turn right onto the road. Sadie walked slowly at first and Daniel concentrated on his breathing. He would not let his fear get the best of him.

4. At first Sadie trotted along the side of the road. There wasn't a house or a person in sight, just wilderness. Daniel thought about his father lying on the ground in pain and squeezed his calves and heels tightly. Sadie obeyed and began to gallop and then run. Daniel leaned forward as Sadie dashed along the side of the road. She did not even flinch when a car sped past them. They had been running for only minutes, but to Daniel it felt like hours. He couldn't stop thinking about his dad. Finally Daniel saw some cars and a streetlight. "That's town!" he shouted. He looked at his watch. He and Sadie had made the journey in only twenty minutes. "There it is!" Daniel shouted when he saw the small hospital.

5. He kissed the top of Sadie's head, dismounted, tied her reins to a post, and ran inside.

Name_____ Date_____

COMMON CORE
STATE STANDARDS
W.4.1–
W.4.10

Opinion/Argument Prompt

Who do you think is a bigger hero, Daniel or Sadie? Support your opinion with details from both Chapter 1 and Chapter 2.

Informative/Explanatory Prompt

Explain why Daniel chooses to ride Sadie instead of Riot or Mandy. Use details from the texts to support your answer.

Narrative Prompt

Write Chapter 3. Tell what happens when Daniel goes into the hospital. Use details from Chapters 1 and 2 to help you. Include characters, descriptions, and dialogue.

COMMON CORE
STATE STANDARDS
W.4.1–
W.4.10

Name_____ Date_____

Read the passages.

Grandmother's Farm

1. Carla could hardly wait to spend the summer at her grandmother's farm. However, after she arrived, she found that she was spending most of her time helping her grandmother with chores. Grandmother did not insist on this, but Carla did not really have anything else to do.

2. While the kids in the neighborhood said hello to her, they did not seem to remember her from the time she spent there in the past. After two weeks, Carla still did not have a real friend.

3. Bored, Carla decided to spend a day at the library reading. When she returned, Gran was in the kitchen cooking dinner. She asked Carla to help her prepare the vegetables, but Carla had never cooked before. Gran handed her a pile of carrots and onions. She taught her how to hold the knife and carefully cut them up. Carla did her best, but the pieces came out ragged and uneven.

4. Baking was more fun. Gran made everything herself— mostly bread and rolls, but sometimes a pie or cookies. Carla loved bread, so Gran showed her how to measure the ingredients. They mixed the dough and kneaded it, pushing and folding and pressing the dough until it felt just right. Then they let it rise. Finally they baked it. After several lessons, Carla could do it by herself. She had just made her first batch of rolls.

5. The next day, Carla was eating lunch at the park and a girl named Meg sat down across from her. "What's that you're eating?" she asked in a surprised voice. "It's just a sandwich," Carla explained, "but I made the roll, so that's why it looks different. Would you like to try a piece?" Meg bit into the bread and said, "Wow, it's really good! How do you make bread?" Carla explained the steps and said, "It's really fun. Maybe you could come over tomorrow, and we could make something together." Meg said that she would love to and would ask her mom.

(continued)

Name_____ Date_____

Common Core
State Standards
W.4.1–
W.4.10

(continued)

6.   The next day, Carla and Meg looked through Gran's old cookbook and found a recipe for cinnamon raisin rolls. As they measured flour, salt, honey, and yeast into the bowl, Gran watched to make sure nothing was forgotten. The girls mixed the dough themselves and took turns kneading it. When it was ready, they sprinkled it with cinnamon and sugar and set it aside to rise. The rolls smelled heavenly as they baked and tasted even better when they were done.

7.   "My dad makes the best chili in the world, Carla," Meg said. "Maybe you can come to my house next week, and he can teach us how to make it!" Carla told Meg that she would love to learn how to make chili.

(continue to next passage)

COMMON CORE
STATE STANDARDS
W.4.1–
W.4.10

Name_____ Date_____

(continued)

Recipe for Friendship

1. Once when I was lonely
2. I took a look around.
3. There were people everywhere
4. but no friends to be found.

5. It might sound easy, making friends,
6. Like falling off a log.
7. But when you're shy it can be
8. more like walking in the fog.

9. My grandma has her recipes
10. For soups and meats and breads.
11. She also knows just what it takes
12. To keep my spirit fed.

13. To make a friend, she told me,
14. Just use my recipe
15. And be yourself and be someone
16. who others like to see.

17. Take kindness, curiosity,
18. and a cheerful attitude.
19. Top it with a smile
20. And a warm and gracious mood.

21. Be sure to add some humor
22. And a lot of loyalty.
23. Include a heap of patience
24. and some generosity.

25. When I mixed it all together
26. I could feel that I had grown.
27. And now I have so many friends
28. I'll never be alone.

Name_____ Date_____

Opinion/Argument Prompt

Do you think Meg follows the "recipe for friendship" described in the poem? Support your opinion with details from the story and the poem.

Informative/Explanatory Prompt

Explain how Gran is like the grandmother in the poem. Use details from the story and the poem to support your explanation.

Narrative Prompt

Write a letter to Carla from the speaker of the poem giving Carla advice on how to make more friends while she is at her grandmother's farm.

COMMON CORE
STATE STANDARDS
W.4.1–
W.4.10

Name_____ Date_____

Read the passages.

Liam Slows the Sun
A Folktale from New Zealand

1. Liam knows how to use magic. He uses his magic for excitement and to help his family.

2. Liam and his family tried to do a great deal of work each day, but the Sun was not cooperating. Lately the Sun raced across the sky and was gone before Liam and his family finished their work. Liam's brothers rose earlier and earlier to hunt and fish, but the days were too short to gather enough food to eat.

3. After much thought, Liam came up with a plan. He would tame the Sun and make him stop racing across the sky. His brothers laughed at the suggestion. "No one can tame the Sun!" they cried. "He will burn you! He will never slow down." They had forgotten about Liam's magic.

4. Liam did not listen to them. He sent all the women to cut flax and bring enormous piles of leaves to the village. He showed them how to braid the flax into strong ropes. Next he tied some of the ropes into nets. Liam picked up his magical wand and led the strongest warriors east. They searched until they found the Sun's resting place and waited outside his cave. Before dawn, the men stretched the net across the cave opening and covered the ropes with leaves. They smeared cool, wet clay all over their bodies to protect themselves from the Sun's heat.

(continued)

Name_____ Date_____

COMMON CORE
STATE STANDARDS
W.4.1–
W.4.10

(continued)

5. Soon the men saw light in the cave and felt the Sun's heat. They worried that Liam's plan would not work. They were blinded by the light and weakened as the air grew hotter. But when Liam yelled "Pull the ropes!" the warriors did, and the net wrapped around the Sun. They held onto the ropes tightly to keep the energetic Sun from racing away.

6. The Sun became angry and fought hard to break free from the net. While the men held the Sun down, Liam ran forward and waved his magic wand at the Sun. Liam used his magic to make the Sun very tired.

7. Liam and the men let the Sun go. Too tired to run, the Sun moved slowly across the sky.

8. Liam and the other warriors returned home. The days were longer now and they could finish their work. Liam and his magic had saved the day.

(continue to next passage)

COMMON CORE
STATE STANDARDS
W.4.1–
W.4.10

Name_____ Date_____

(continued)

Phaethon and the Sun Chariot
A Myth from Ancient Greece

1.   Phaethon was very unhappy. He lived with his sisters and his mother, and his father was Helios, the sun god. But Helios was too busy to visit, and Phaethon's friends did not believe his father was the sun god. This made Phaethon sad, so his mother sent him to visit Helios. Phaethon traveled a long time before he finally arrived at the home of his father.

2.   Helios's job was to drive the shining sun chariot across the sky each day. Without Helios to travel above Earth, the world would be dark and cold. He welcomed his son and offered Phaethon a gift—the boy could ask for one wish, and Helios would grant it. Phaethon thought that if he rode across the sky in the sun chariot, everyone would know he was the son of Helios. His wish was to drive the chariot. Now his father was worried. Helios asked Phaethon to make a different wish because driving the sun chariot was dangerous. But Phaethon was stubborn—he demanded to drive the chariot.

3.   Helios's sister, Eos, began to open the curtain in the east to let the day begin. Helios had the fire-breathing horses hitched to the golden chariot and told Phaethon to hold the reins tightly. Helios spread oil on Phaethon's face to protect him from the heat, and set his crown of rays on the boy's head.

4.   Suddenly the horses raced into the sky, and Phaethon was not strong enough to control them. They first soared too high, burning the heavens and creating the Milky Way. Then they flew very low. Earth was burning from the horses' fiery breath. This created many deserts.

5.   Phaethon was nearly blind from the blazing light. Terrified, he dropped the reins. As the horses flew on, people on the ground cried out in fear and pain. Zeus, the king of the gods, heard their screams and threw a bolt of lightning that caused Phaethon and the sun chariot to crash into a river. Zeus turned Phaethon's sisters into poplar trees so they would have to stand by the river forever and guard their brother.

Name_____ Date_____

COMMON CORE
STATE STANDARDS
W.4.1–
W.4.10

Opinion/Argument Prompt

Which story about the sun do you like better, "Liam Slows the Sun" or "Phaethon and the Sun Chariot"? Support your opinion with reasons from the texts.

Informative/Explanatory Prompt

How are Liam and Phaethon different? Use reasons from both texts to support your explanation.

Narrative Prompt

Imagine that Liam and Helios met. Write a story about what they would say and do. Include dialogue in which they discuss how they helped bring daylight to the world.

COMMON CORE
STATE STANDARDS
W.4.1–
W.4.10

Name_____ Date_____

Read the passages.

The Fox and the Grapes
An Adaptation of Aesop's Fable

1. The sun was beating down on Fox's head. It was a hot summer day, and he was thirsty and hungry. Fox scampered through the forest, sniffing the ground for water, but the creek was dry.

2. "Oh, my tongue is so dry," he muttered. "And my stomach is so empty that it grumbles." Fox raised his head and sniffed. "Oh my goodness, do I smell grapes? Juicy grapes would be wonderful right now."

3. Suddenly Fox found he had the energy to run. He raced swiftly up a hill, soared over a fence, and landed in a fruit orchard. He sniffed again. Oh, such deliciousness, where were the grapes?

4. He lifted his head high and noticed that he was standing below a vine. There, gently swinging in the light breeze, were juicy bunches of grapes. Even in the summer's heat, Fox could feel his mouth watering.

5. Fox crouched low and gave a mighty leap. His jaws snapped at the grapes, but he missed them. He tried again, but he still could not reach the grapes. "Who is responsible for this?" he grumbled. "Why would someone put grapes up so high that I can't reach them?"

6. Angry, Fox circled the orchard. He began to run and then leaped as high as he could. He tried again and again, but then he dropped to the ground, panting. "Vines are such a nuisance," he murmured.

(continued)

Name_____ Date_____

COMMON CORE
STATE STANDARDS
W.4.1–
W.4.10

(continued)

7. The weary fox rolled onto his back and studied the orchard. The vine was high, but it was close to the fence that he had leaped over earlier. Maybe if he found a high spot where he could jump, he would reach the grapes.

8. He stood and scrambled onto the wooden fence. He wobbled as he got his balance. Gazing steadily at the pretty purple grapes, Fox paused and then bounded into the sky. He leaped as high as he could and stretched his neck as far as he could reach, but again, his teeth missed the grapes.

9. Fox landed in a heap on the hot, dusty ground. For a long time, he did not move. He listened to the grumble in his stomach and felt the hot sun on his head. Finally he stood up and approached the vine.

10. Glaring at the grapes, Fox stomped his foot. "I don't want any silly old grapes anyway," he huffed. "In fact, I think those grapes are probably sour."

11. Then Fox turned and trudged away, never looking back.

(continue to next passage)

COMMON CORE
STATE STANDARDS
W.4.1–
W.4.10

Name_____ Date_____

(continued)

The Fisherman and the Little Fish
An Adaptation of Aesop's Fable

1. A fisherman and his wife lived on the banks of a river. Carlos, the fisherman, walked each day to the water's edge to cast his net into the river.

2. Some days Carlos caught only a few fish. On these days, he carried the fish home to his wife, Tia. Other days the fisherman's net was filled with wiggling fish. If he caught more than he and Tia could eat, Carlos sold the fish at the market.

3. The fisherman and his wife were very happy. If the weather was good, they tended a garden of tomatoes, cabbage, and lettuce. When the summer was dry, however, they had to rely on the river to provide fish.

4. One summer when there was very little rain, Carlos threw his net into the river. He waited for the net to sink and settle, and then he began to pull the ropes and gather it. But the empty net snagged on the rocks because the river was shallow. Carlos fished all morning, but he caught nothing.

5. "We have no fish today, Tia," Carlos grumbled.

6. "Here," said Tia. "Have a fresh tomato from the garden. I will slice some bread for your lunch. Then you will try again."

7. Carlos sighed, but after eating he returned to the river. The next time he pulled in the net, a glistening little fish wiggled in it.

8. "Please release me, good sir!" cried the little fish. "Let me go and I will grow larger. Then you can catch me and have a fine meal."

9. Carlos was very surprised. No fish had ever spoken to him before.

10. "Tia is hungry today," said Carlos. "Only a fool would take a chance on a better catch in the future and throw away his dinner." With that, Carlos carried the fish home to his wife, and after dinner they once again danced around their kitchen.

Name_____ Date_____

COMMON CORE
STATE STANDARDS
W.4.1–
W.4.10

Opinion/Argument Prompt

Do you agree with the decisions Fox and Carlos make? Why or why not? Support your opinion with details from the texts.

Informative/Explanatory Prompt

What can you tell about Fox from the story? What can you tell about Carlos? Use details from both stories to support your opinions.

Narrative Prompt

Write a new ending to each story that tells about Fox getting the grapes and Carlos releasing the fish.

Common Core
State Standards

W.4.1–
W.4.10

Name_____ Date_____

Read the passages.

The Case of the Missing Necklace

1. Heather took off the necklace her grandmother had given her for her birthday and put it in her jewelry box. She then shut the jewelry box drawer, turned out the lights, and crawled into bed.

2. She thought about wearing the necklace to school the next day but decided against it. She remembered that she had gym class. "I better not wear it," she said to herself. "It might get broken." Then she closed the door to her room and headed to the kitchen for breakfast.

3. After school, Heather and her best friend Jada were in her room quizzing each other on their spelling words. "Did you see the necklace my grandmother gave me?" she asked Jada, who shook her head. "It's my favorite thing in the whole world. I just love it."

4. Heather gasped when she opened the jewelry box drawer. "It's gone!" she exclaimed. "Someone must have taken it! I'm positive that I put the necklace in here last night before I went to bed."

5. Heather asked her mother, father, and older brother Ryan if they had seen the necklace, but none of them had. Then she and Jada searched the house. They finally found the necklace under the sofa in the living room.

6. "It must have fallen off you when you were wearing it," Heather's mother concluded.

7. Heather shook her head. "I am absolutely positive that I put it in my jewelry box. I even closed the door to my room this morning. Come to think of it, the door was open when I came home. Were you in there?" Heather asked her mom, who said that she had not been in her daughter's room that day.

8. "I think we have a mystery to solve," said Jada.

(continued)

Name_____ Date_____

COMMON CORE
STATE STANDARDS
W.4.1–
W.4.10

(continued)

9. Heather and Jada enjoyed solving mysteries. The girls frequently read the same mystery novels at the same time, so they could try to figure out "who done it." Their friends at school often asked for their help in solving real-life mysteries. "I think we should start by taking a careful look at my room," suggested Heather.

10. "I wish we could dust for fingerprints," Jada said as Heather picked up the jewelry box and looked carefully at the dresser underneath.

11. "Maybe the thief dropped something or left behind a clue that will help us figure out his or her identify," Heather said and set the jewelry box back in its place. Then the girls looked under the bed and in the closet, but they didn't find a single clue.

12. Frustrated, Heather plopped on her bed and Jada sat beside her. Just then Heather noticed that the doorknob on her door was turning. Then the door opened, but no one stepped inside. Heather stood up and saw Whiskers, her family's cat, standing in front of the door.

13. "Your cat just opened the door!" Jada exclaimed. Heather was not surprised. She had seen Whiskers use his long front legs and paws to do this before.

14. Then the two girls watched in amazement as Whiskers jumped up onto Heather's dresser and made his way to her jewelry box. He pulled open a drawer and looked inside. Heather's mouth hung open as she watched him dash out of her room with a shiny bracelet in his mouth.

15. "Well, I think we just solved the case of the missing necklace!" Jada said and laughed.

(continue to next passage)

COMMON CORE
STATE STANDARDS
W.4.1–
W.4.10

Name_____ Date_____

(continued)

The Case of the Missing Homework

1.   Jada told her best friend Heather about her problem. "I can't believe this happened again. I did my homework last night but it wasn't in my folder today so I couldn't hand it in."

2.   "This is a mystery for sure," Heather concluded. "Maybe if we retrace your steps, we can figure out what happened."

3.   "Each night, I do my homework at this desk in my room," Jada said and pointed to the desk. "Then I put my homework for Mrs. Walker's class in this folder."

4.   "Where do you put the folder when you're finished?" Heather asked.

5.   "I put it on my desk with my books. Then I put everything in my backpack in the morning."

6.   "So it's likely that the thief comes into your room after you've finished your homework and takes it out of your folder," Heather explained. "Who has access to your room?"

7.   "Just my parents, sisters, and brother. But they wouldn't try to get me in trouble," Jada said.

8.   "Maybe it's someone who doesn't know taking papers out of your folder will get you into trouble. The thief might be someone very young."

9.   Jada's eyes widened. "Tiara loves to come into my room. She sometimes takes pens and pencils."

10.   Jada left her room and came back with her three-year-old sister. "Tiara, Heather and I want to ask you something but you're not in any trouble, okay?" The little girl nodded. "Do you ever take papers out of this folder on my desk?" Jada asked.

11.   "Just to color them," Tiara replied.

12.   "Well, I think I need to put my homework in my backpack right away from now on," Jada said.

13.   "The super sleuths have done it again! The mystery is solved," Heather said and cheered.

Common Core Writing to Texts Grade 4 • ©2014 Newmark Learning, LLC

Name_____ Date_____

COMMON CORE
STATE STANDARDS
W.4.1–
W.4.10

Opinion/Argument Prompt

**Which mystery do you think was more difficult to solve,
"The Case of the Missing Necklace" or "The Case of the
Missing Homework"? Support your opinion with reasons from
both stories.**

Informative/Explanatory Prompt

**Summarize the problem and solution in each story. Be sure to
include specific details from the texts.**

Narrative Prompt

**Write a story in which Jada and Heather solve "The Case of
the Missing Hamster." Use text details about the girls' lives
and personalities to help you.**

COMMON CORE
STATE STANDARDS

W.4.1–
W.4.10

Name_____ Date_____

Read the passages.

Why We Should Not Have School Uniforms

1. Dear School Board Members,

2.   My name is Keisha Hamilton, and I am a fourth-grade student at Miller Avenue School. I am writing about the new uniforms you may soon require students to wear to school. Requiring us to wear school uniforms is not a good idea.

3.   Uniforms make everyone look the same—but we are not the same. We are all individuals with unique personalities and likes and dislikes. Our clothing is one way we express our personalities. Here are a few examples.

4.   My brother likes baseball. Each day he likes to wear a different T-shirt from one of his favorite teams. If my brother must wear a uniform, no one will know which baseball teams are his favorites.

5.   My best friend Sara Jane takes ballet lessons and likes to wear ballet clothes to school. She doesn't wear her costumes or her toe shoes. But she does wear ballet leotards and tights with her jeans. She says her outfits make her feel more like a dancer even when she is doing math. If she has to wear a uniform, she won't be able to express her personality this way in school.

6.   As for me, I love to skateboard. I skateboard as often as I can before and after school. I wear my skateboarding clothes to school. If I have to wear a uniform, I will have to go home and change my clothes before skateboarding. This would be a problem for me.

(continued)

Name_____ Date_____

COMMON CORE
STATE STANDARDS
W.4.1–
W.4.10

(continued)

7. Skateboarding is great exercise but if I have to go all the way home to change each day, I might be tempted to skip skateboarding and watch television instead. Having to wear a school uniform would affect my healthy lifestyle.

8. School uniforms also do not look nice. I hope I don't offend anyone by writing this, but it's true. If uniforms looked nice, everybody would be wearing them. However, the only students who wear them do so because it's required.

9. Please don't force us to wear school uniforms. We want the freedom to use our clothes to express our personalities. We want to wear clothes that are comfortable and look nice.

10. Sincerely yours,

11. Keisha Hamilton

(continue to next passage)

COMMON CORE
STATE STANDARDS
W.4.1–
W.4.10

Name_____ Date_____

(continued)

Why We Should Have School Uniforms

1. Dear Members of the School Board,

2. I realize that I am in the minority and that many of my classmates will disagree with me. However, I think the students in our school should wear uniforms. My name is Nathan Ford, and I have three brothers and two sisters. My parents both work full time, so my siblings and I have to help out at home.

3. My brother Pete and I are in charge of the laundry. As you can imagine, with so many children, we have many loads of clothes to wash! If our school required us to wear uniforms, it would reduce the number of loads of laundry we have to do. My brothers and sisters and I could wear the same uniform two days in a row and no one would notice.

4. Our parents would also save money if we were required to wear uniforms. Instead of buying many school clothes for us, they would only have to buy a few uniforms. Of course, we have to wear clothes when we are not at school, but we don't feel pressure at home to wear trendy clothes. My siblings and I often wear old sweatshirts and jeans at home. If we dressed liked this at school, kids might make fun of us.

5. Lastly, our parents sacrifice so that we can all wear trendy clothing. However, even with sacrifice, some families can't afford this kind of clothing. It is better for the kids from these families if we all wear uniforms. The kids who have the trendy clothes won't be able to look down on them because their families can't afford such clothing.

6. Thanks for considering my point of view.

7. Yours truly,

8. Nathan Ford

Name_____ Date_____

COMMON CORE
STATE STANDARDS
W.4.1–
W.4.10

Opinion/Argument Prompt

Which letter do you think is more likely to change the minds of readers? Why? Support your opinion with evidence from the texts.

Informative/Explanatory Prompt

Suppose that the school board members decide to require students to wear school uniforms. Write a speech that the school principal might make to inform students of this decision. Discuss the points made in each letter.

Narrative Prompt

Imagine that Nathan and Keisha got in an argument at recess about the school uniform issue. Write a story about what would happen. Use details from their speeches to help you.

COMMON CORE
STATE STANDARDS
W.4.1–
W.4.10

Name_____ Date_____

Read the passages.

Our Unusual Earth

1.   Our solar system has eight planets. The four inner planets are closer to the sun. These planets are Mercury, Venus, Earth, and Mars. The four outer planets are farther from the sun. These planets are Jupiter, Saturn, Uranus, and Neptune. Of the eight planets, only one can support life— the only planet in our solar system that is known to support life is Earth.

Atmosphere

2.   Life on Earth is possible because of the atmosphere. The atmosphere is the layer of air and gases that surround Earth. The atmosphere of Earth is made up mostly of nitrogen and oxygen. It has other gases in small amounts too. These substances protect Earth and allow living things to breathe and thrive.

Surface

3.   Earth is also the only planet that is known to have liquid water on its surface. Water is important for life because most living things cannot live without it. Water covers almost 70 percent of Earth's surface. Much of this water is in oceans, rivers, and lakes. There is water in the air in the form of water vapor. There is also water under the ice caps and glaciers, in the ground, and even in living beings, like you!

4.   The other 30 percent of Earth's surface is made of rock. That's why the four inner planets are sometimes called the terrestrial, or rocky, planets. The outer planets are different because they are made of gas instead of rock.

(continued)

Name_____ Date_____

Common Core
State Standards
W.4.1–
W.4.10

(continued)

Orbit

5.   Earth travels around the sun in a path called an orbit. It takes about 365 days, or one year, for Earth to orbit around the sun. Earth also has a space object in its orbit—the moon. The moon orbits Earth in the same way that Earth orbits the sun. The moon's official name is Luna. The moon takes about 28 days to orbit around Earth.

6.   As Earth orbits around the sun, it also turns in place, or rotates, on its axis. Earth's axis is an imaginary line that runs through the center of the planet. One end of the line is at the North Pole, and the other end is at the South Pole. It takes about 24 hours for Earth to rotate one time along this line. As Earth rotates, the side facing the sun experiences day. The side facing away from the sun experiences night.

Fast Facts About Earth

Diameter:	7,926 miles (12,760 km)
Distance from sun:	93 million miles (149,600,000 km)
Length of orbit around sun:	365 days
Number/names of moons:	1/Luna
Temperature:	Average 45°F (7.2°C)
Atmosphere:	Mostly nitrogen and oxygen
Surface features:	Rocky with liquid water (70%)

(continue to next passage)

COMMON CORE
STATE STANDARDS
W.4.1–
W.4.10

Name_____ Date_____

(continued)

Our Neighbor Mars

1. Mars is the fourth planet from the sun. Because Earth is the third planet from the sun, Mars is practically our next-door neighbor! Mars is an inner planet, like Earth. However, Mars is quite a different place.

2. One of the biggest differences between Earth and Mars is the atmosphere. Earth's rich atmosphere contains mostly nitrogen and oxygen gases. These gases allow living things to breathe. The atmosphere on Mars, on the other hand, has very little oxygen or nitrogen. Instead, it is very thin and made up mostly of carbon dioxide and other gases. These gases do not support life.

3. Scientists believe that Mars may have once had rivers, lakes, and even an ocean. However, that water has vanished. Scientists think it may have evaporated, or disappeared, into the atmosphere. Some of the water may still be frozen under ice caps or trapped underground.

4. The weather on Mars is much more extreme than the weather on Earth. Looking through powerful telescopes, scientists can see that the planet has fierce wind storms. These storms sometimes last for months at a time. The storms whip up the fine red dust that covers the surface of the planet. That's why Mars is sometimes called the Red Planet.

5. Mars may be Earth's closest neighbor, but it is a much colder place. Like Earth, the temperature probably varies from day to night and from place to place. However, scientists believe the temperature on Mars is usually well below zero.

6. Almost fifty years ago, scientists began sending unmanned spacecraft to Mars. Early crafts flew past Mars and took photos. In 2012, scientists landed an unmanned laboratory, *Curiosity*, on Mars. *Curiosity* has been sending back data and images ever since. Scientists are hoping that this laboratory will help them learn much more about the Red Planet, Earth's closest neighbor.

Name_____ Date_____

COMMON CORE
STATE STANDARDS
W.4.1–
W.4.10

Opinion/Argument Prompt

Do you think people will one day live on Mars? Why or why not? Support your opinion with reasons from both texts.

Informative/Explanatory Prompt

Explain how Earth and Mars are alike and different. Use specific examples from both texts to support your explanation.

Narrative Prompt

Imagine you are on a spacecraft that just landed on Mars. Write a story describing what it is like on the Red Planet. Include how Mars is different from Earth. Use details from both texts.

COMMON CORE
STATE STANDARDS
W.4.1–
W.4.10

Name_____ Date_____

Read the passages.

The Beautiful Emerald Isle

1.   Ireland has a special nickname. It's called the Emerald Isle. The color emerald is bright green, and Ireland is a very green place. Ireland is home to lush, rolling green fields and hills and plenty of bright green grass and moss. Because it rains often, plants grow very well there. In Ireland, it's not unusual to have both sunny and rainy weather on the same day. The frequent misty rain also keeps the temperature cool. The hottest days in Ireland are only about 60 degrees.

Life in Ireland

2.   Ireland is home to many storytellers. These people like to share Irish legends about rainbows and leprechauns. Many poets and authors have also told stories about Ireland and its people. Singers and songwriters have created music about Ireland, too.

3.   Many people in Ireland enjoy life in the country. Ireland has few trees and is mostly made up of large plains between low mountains. So much open space makes Ireland a great place for farm animals. Farmers have grown crops in Ireland throughout the country's history.

4.   Other people live in cities such as Dublin, which is the capital. Dublin is also oldest city in Ireland. The River Liffey divides the city in half. Most of the buildings in Dublin are very old. Some are even castles. Many people visit Dublin to see its fairy-tale-like castles and cobblestone streets. They also visit the city's many museums, parks, and gardens.

Did you know . . .
- There are no wild snakes in Ireland. Because the country is an island, wild snakes have never made it there.

- According to a legend, if you kiss a famous stone in Blarney Castle, you will receive "the gift of gab."

- The four-leaf clover is an important symbol of good luck in Ireland.

- According to another legend, if you can catch a leprechaun, he will show you where he keeps his pot of gold.

(continue to next passage)

Name_____ Date_____

COMMON CORE
STATE STANDARDS
W.4.1–
W.4.10

(continued)

Sherman School News

FEBRUARY 28

Interview with Lindy Hall
by Emily Porter

1. **Question: What can you tell us about yourself and your family?**

2. **Answer:** I am a ten-year-old girl, and I have a younger brother named Andrew who is seven years old. We live with Mam and Da in Dublin, Ireland.

3. **Question: What does your house look like?**

4. **Answer:** Our house is small and attached to other homes on both sides. Our house is actually part of a long building that stretches the entire length of the street. The building is divided into different houses and each house has its own front door and picture window. The front of each house is painted a different color and each front door is brightly painted, too. Our house is red brick with a white door. Da planted pretty flowers near the entrance.

(continued)

COMMON CORE
STATE STANDARDS
W.4.1–
W.4.10

Name_____ Date_____

(continued)

Sherman School News

FEBRUARY 28

---

5. **Question: What else can you tell us about your home and neighborhood?**

6. **Answer:** Our home is small, but it is quite comfortable. Downstairs we have a parlor and a kitchen. Upstairs we have three small bedrooms. At the end of our street is an old factory. It is empty now, but years ago people built ships there. We can also walk to stores and restaurants. Sometimes Mam gives me money to get something for her from the store.

7. **Question: What kinds of food do you like to eat?**

8. **Answer:** Mam is a good cook, and she likes to make vegetable stew and soup. Sometimes for a treat, we order food from the take-away, a restaurant where you call up and place an order but you do not eat there; you pick up your food and take it home with you to eat. Andrew likes to order pizza from the take-away. I like to order chips made from fried potatoes. Of course, we often have tea and biscuits. We love sweeties.

9. **Question: Do you go to school?**

10. **Answer:** Oh, yes, we go to school near our house. Andrew walks to school with his chums and I walk with mine. We wear school uniforms. Our school is strict, and we have a great deal of schoolwork to do. It's important to do well in school because we must earn points that will let us take tests to get into a university. If we do not have enough points, we will not be allowed to take the test for the university of our liking. Andrew and I do not want that to happen to us, so we are quite serious about our studies in class. Still, we have fun with our chums in the schoolyard.

Common Core Writing to Texts Grade 4 • ©2014 Newmark Learning, LLC

Name_____ Date_____

COMMON CORE
STATE STANDARDS
W.4.1–
W.4.10

Opinion/Argument Prompt

Do you think Ireland would be a nice place to live or visit? Why or why not? Support your opinion with details from the texts.

Informative/Explanatory Prompt

Explain what life is like in Dublin. Use details from both texts to support your explanation.

Narrative Prompt

Write a letter to Lindy telling her what your life is like in the United States. Explain how it is alike and different from her life in Ireland.

COMMON CORE
STATE STANDARDS

W.4.1–
W.4.10

Name_____ Date_____

Read the passages.

We Should Build a Skatepark

1.   Greetings,

2.   My name is Eddie Carver, and I am the parent of a twelve-year-old boy, Scott. I am the president of our town's skatepark committee. I am here tonight to tell you why we need to build a skatepark in our town.

3.   Our committee surveyed the middle and high school students in our town's schools. We estimate that at least 400 of our students are already skateboarders. Another 200 students expressed an interest in learning to skateboard.

4.   Skateboarding is a great pastime. Because of skateboarding icons such as Tony Hawk, skateboarding has become immensely popular. It is a great way for kids to gather together to exercise and socialize. To skateboard correctly and safely, however, kids really need to be at a skatepark. In case you are unfamiliar with the sport, skateparks have special bowls and ramps. The idea is that kids can skateboard without having to use their feet to push on the ground. Skateboarders master stunts such as ollies and kickflips. They try to perfect twists and flips. Many skateboarders take lessons at skateparks.

5.   Right now our town has no safe place for kids to skateboard. They skateboard on roads, in parking lots, and on sidewalks. They skateboard in dangerous places such as on loading docks, decks, and stair rails. Needless to say, they are not welcome in these places. People are afraid that skateboarders will crash into them or their vehicles. We have visited other towns that have skateparks. They do not have these problems because kids have a safe place to go.

(continued)

Name_____ Date_____

(continued)

6.   We would like to build the skatepark in the back section of Memorial Park near our town's square. We feel that building the park in this area will ensure that skateboarders will not bother citizens walking in the park. The skatepark will also have a pavilion where people can sit and watch the skateboarders. We plan to install vending machines and will use the money they earn to help maintain the skatepark.

7.   We plan to install a ten-foot fence surrounding the park and motion detectors to alert police if someone is in the park after it is closed. Skateboarders will be granted a pass to the park. If they do not follow the rules of conduct, they will lose their pass temporarily. Repeated violations will result in a permanent loss of a skateboarding pass. Children under nine must be accompanied by a parent.

8.   I hope you will support us in our mission to give our kids a safe place to exercise. We have secured public and private grant money to build the park. Many of our town's skateboarders have promised to volunteer their time to assist in the construction of the park. The cost to our city will be minimal.

9.   Thank you for your time.

(continue to next passage)

COMMON CORE
STATE STANDARDS
W.4.1–
W.4.10

Name_____ Date_____

(continued)

We Should Not Build a Skatepark

1. Good evening.

2. My name is Regina Coleman. I would like to speak to you about the skatepark our town may build. I would like to begin by saying that I am the mother of five children and a member of the town council.

3. I am against the construction of the skatepark mainly because our town simply cannot afford it. Mr. Carver was kind enough to explain that his committee has secured grants to pay for most of the cost to build the park. As you know, our town is strapped for funds at the moment. We have recently laid off firefighters and police officers.

4. There are other costs associated with skateparks in addition to construction. Insurance for a skatepark is very expensive. Even if our town requires skateboarders to wear helmets and kneepads, we still can't afford the monthly insurance bill. Money is also needed to maintain a skatepark. These parks must be routinely inspected for wear and tear. Their surface needs to be swept and mopped each day. Even dust can make the surface slippery. A skateboarder may be injured if the surface becomes dusty. Who is going to pay to maintain the park?

5. Mr. Carver and his committee have not mentioned installing bathrooms or drinking fountains in the park. Without bathrooms, kids are going to use facilities in nearby restaurants and stores. These facilities are meant for customers. Business owners and their customers will be annoyed if skateboarders routinely use them.

6. Perhaps in the future when our town has more money, we can build a skatepark with drinking fountains and bathrooms, and we will be able to afford the daily maintenance. However, for now, the only responsible choice is to say "no" to the skatepark.

7. Thank you.

Common Core Writing to Texts Grade 4 • ©2014 Newmark Learning, LLC

Name_____ Date_____

Common Core
State Standards
W.4.1–
W.4.10

Opinion/Argument Prompt

Do you think this town should build a skatepark? Why or why not? Support your opinion with details from both texts.

Informative/Explanatory Prompt

Summarize the position of each speaker. Use details from each speech to build your summary.

Narrative Prompt

Imagine that the town decides to build a skatepark. Write a story about what happens on opening day. Include details and people from both speeches.

COMMON CORE
STATE STANDARDS
W.4.1–
W.4.10

Name_____ Date_____

Read the passages.

The Daily Herald

July 2, 1874

Zoo Grand Opening!

1. Philadelphia—The Philadelphia Zoo opened its gates for the first time yesterday. It is the first zoo in the United States. More than 3,000 visitors were welcomed by a brass band.

2. Visitors arrived at the zoo for its much-anticipated opening day in a variety of ways. Many traveled by foot or in horse-drawn carriages. Others arrived in packed streetcars. Yet most visitors traveled to the zoo in a steamboat on the Schuylkill River. The steamboat was the most direct way to get to the zoo from downtown.

3. The Philadelphia Zoo sits on 33 acres of land near the banks of the Schuylkill River at 3400 West Girard Avenue. Admission to the zoo is 25 cents for adults and 10 cents for children.

4. The mission of the Philadelphia Zoo is to study and protect animals throughout the world. The zoo houses more than 800 animals, including giraffes, cheetahs, and hippos. Visitors also had a chance to see a langur, a leaf-eating monkey, and a marmoset.

5. The creators of the zoo designed some of the displays to look like the animals' natural homes in the wild. For example, the African Plains display is home to the zoo's elephants and rhinos. The Australian display is home to kangaroos.

6. Other attractions include Bear Country, which features a 200,000-gallon pool for the zoo's polar bears. Visitors can enjoy seeing more than 100 species of birds. The Philadelphia Zoo also has some rare animals such as a pair of white lions, Jezebel and Vinkel, and clouded leopards.

(continued)

Common Core Writing to Texts Grade 4 • ©2014 Newmark Learning, LLC

Name_____ Date_____

(continued)

_____

_____

_____

7. "This is truly amazing," said William Sanders, one of the zoo's first visitors on opening day. "Without this zoo, none of us would ever have a chance to see animals like this. We would not, for example, get to see an elephant. This zoo not only gives us a chance to see these exotic animals, but it also teaches us about them."

8. Surprisingly, the Philadelphia Zoo was founded 15 years before it opened. A charter, a document establishing the zoo, was approved and signed in March 1859. However, because of the Civil War, the opening of the zoo was delayed for 15 years.

9. Visitors of the zoo are anticipating the opening of the Girard Avenue Bridge in two days. The bridge extends Girard Avenue over East River Drive, the Schuylkill River, the Schuylkill Canal, and West River Drive. The bridge is expected to make it much easier for visitors to get to the zoo.

(continue to next passage)

COMMON CORE
STATE STANDARDS
W.4.1–
W.4.10

Name_____ Date_____

(continued)

July 1, 1874
(journal entry, Sarah Parker)

1. I had the most amazing day today! Harold, the children, and I rose early this morning and headed downtown. We were very excited because we were going to attend opening day at the Philadelphia Zoo, the first zoo in the United States!

2. When we made it downtown, we waited in a long line to get onto a steamboat. This steamboat, which traveled along the Schuylkill River, would take us directly to the zoo. We were a bit disappointed that so many people had also opted to take the steamboat, but we did not let this dampen our enthusiasm.

3. After about fifteen minutes, the steamboat landed at the zoo's wharf, and we made our way to the entrance of the zoo. Many flags blew in the breeze, and we could hear a band playing inside the gates. "Wow," little Richard said when he saw the large iron gates at the zoo's entrance. "Look how big they are!"

4. It was so crowded inside the zoo that I had to hold the children's hands tightly to make sure they did not get lost. People scurried along trying to see as many animals as possible. We headed first to Bear Country because both Richard and Amelia wanted to see a real bear. Up until now, we had only seen illustrations of bears. The children enjoyed seeing the polar bears swim in the gigantic pool. The walls of the pool are glass, so we could see the bears swimming underwater. It was truly spectacular.

5. Harold and I wanted to see the birds next. We saw so many colorful parrots that I simply can't remember them all. After this, we stopped to take a break and get something to eat.

6. The Philadelphia Zoo is an amazing place! I never dreamed that I would actually see an elephant and a rhino unless I went on a safari in Africa. Yet, thanks to the Philadelphia Zoo, I was able to see them.

Common Core Writing to Texts Grade 4 • ©2014 Newmark Learning, LLC

Name_____ Date_____

COMMON CORE
STATE STANDARDS
W.4.1–
W.4.10

Opinion/Argument Prompt

Do you think zoos like the Philadelphia Zoo are important? Why or why not? Support your opinion with reasons from both texts.

Informative/Explanatory Prompt

Explain why people traveled to the zoo on a steamboat and what it was like to travel this way. Support your explanation with details from both texts.

Narrative Prompt

Imagine Sarah Parker met William Sanders, the man interviewed for the newspaper article. Write a dialogue in which they discuss their first day at the zoo.

119

COMMON CORE
STATE STANDARDS

W.4.1
W.4.4
W.4.5

Name_____ Date_____

Opinion/Argument Organizer

My Opinion:

Reason 1:	**Reason 2:**	**Reason 3:**
Supporting Details:	**Supporting Details:**	**Supporting Details:**

My Opinion Restated (Conclusion):

COMMON CORE
STATE STANDARDS
W.4.1
W.4.4
W.4.5

Name_____ Date_____

Opinion/Argument Organizer

My Opinion:

Text 1:	**Text 2:**
Reason 1:	**Reason 1:**
Supporting Evidence:	**Supporting Evidence:**
Reason 2:	**Reason 2:**
Supporting Evidence:	**Supporting Evidence:**

My Conclusion:

COMMON CORE
STATE STANDARDS
W.4.2
W.4.4
W.4.5

Name_____ Date_____

Informative/Explanatory Organizer

Topic:

_____

Main Idea 1:

Supporting Details:

1.

2.

3.

Main Idea 2:

Supporting Details:

1.

2.

3.

Name_____ Date_____

COMMON CORE
STATE STANDARDS
W.4.2
W.4.4
W.4.5

Informative/Explanatory Organizer

Text 1:   **Both**   **Text 2:**

_____   _____

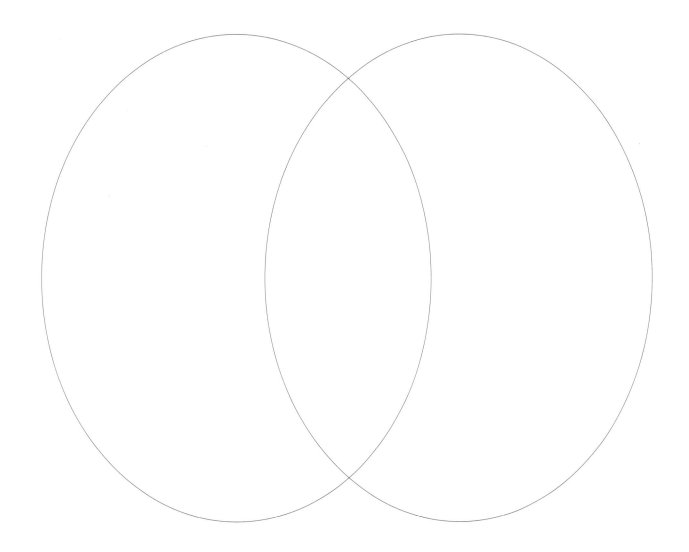

COMMON CORE
STATE STANDARDS

W.4.3

W.4.4

W.4.5

Name_____ Date_____

Narrative Organizer

Sequence of Events

COMMON CORE
STATE STANDARDS
W.4.3
W.4.4
W.4.5

Name_____ Date_____

Narrative Organizer

Characters:

Setting:

Goal/Problem/Conflict:

Details from Stories I Read:

New Events:

Ending/Resolution:

Name_____ Date_____

Common Core
State Standards

**W.4.1–
W.4.5**

Name_____ Date_____

✔ Writing Checklist: Opinion/Argument

❏ I introduced the topic.

❏ I stated a strong opinion, position, or point of view.

❏ I used well-organized reasons to support my opinion.

❏ I supported my reasons with facts and details.

❏ I used linking words and phrases to connect my opinion and reasons, such as *for instance*, *in order to*, and *in addition*.

❏ I ended with a conclusion that sums up and supports my position.

❏ I used correct grammar.

❏ I used correct capitalization, punctuation, and spelling.

✔ Writing Checklist: Informative/Explanatory

❏ I started with a clear topic statement.

❏ I grouped related information in paragraphs.

❏ I developed my topic with facts, definitions, concrete details, quotations, or other information and examples from the text.

❏ I linked ideas and information effectively using words, phrases, and clauses.

❏ I used precise language and terminology to explain the topic.

❏ I wrote a conclusion related to the information I presented.

❏ I reviewed my writing for good grammar.

❏ I reviewed my writing for capitalization, punctuation, and spelling.

COMMON CORE
STATE STANDARDS

W.4.1–
W.4.5

Name_____ Date_____

✔ Writing Checklist: Narrative

- ❏ I established a setting or situation for my narrative.

- ❏ I introduced a narrator and/or characters.

- ❏ I organized my narrative into a sequence of unfolding events.

- ❏ I used dialogue and description to develop events and show how characters respond to them.

- ❏ I used transitional words to show my sequence of events.

- ❏ I used concrete words and phrases and sensory details to describe events.

- ❏ I wrote a conclusion to the events in my narrative.

- ❏ I reviewed my writing for capitalization, punctuation, and spelling.

Rubrics and Assessments

Using the Rubrics to Assess Students and Differentiate Instruction

Use the Evaluation Rubrics on the next page to guide your assessment of students' responses. The rubrics are based on the Common Core State Standards for writing. Similar rubrics will be used by evaluators to score new standardized assessments.

After scoring students' writing, refer to the differentiated rubrics on pages 130–135. These are designed to help you differentiate your interactions and instruction to match students' needs. For each score a student receives in the Evaluation Rubrics, responsive prompts are provided to support writers. These gradual-release prompts scaffold writers toward mastery of each writing type.

• For a score of 1, use the Goal Oriented prompts.

• For a score of 2, use the Directive and Corrective Feedback prompts.

• For a score of 3, use the Self-Monitoring and Reflection prompts.

• For a score of 4, use the Validating and Confirming prompts.

Using Technology

If you choose to have students use computers to write and revise their work, consider these ways to support online collaboration and digital publishing:

• Google Drive facilitates collaboration and allows teachers and peers to provide real-time feedback on writing pieces.

• Wikis enable students to share their writing around a common topic.

• Audio tools enable students to record their works (podcasts) for others to hear on a safe sharing platform.

• Student writing can be enriched with images, audio, and video.

Evaluation Rubrics

Student _____   Grade _____

Teacher _____   Date _____

Opinion/Argument

Traits	1	2	3	4
The writer states a strong opinion, position, or point of view.				
The writer supplies well-organized reasons that support his or her opinion using facts, concrete examples, and supporting evidence from the text.				
The writer links opinions and reasons using words, phrases, and clauses.				
The writer provides a concluding statement or section.				
The writer demonstrates command of grade-appropriate conventions of standard English.				

Informative/Explanatory

Traits	1	2	3	4
The writer introduces his or her topic with a main idea statement.				
The writer uses facts, definitions, and details to develop his or her points.				
The writer groups related information together.				
The writer uses linking words and phrases to connect ideas within categories of information.				
The writer provides a concluding statement or section.				
The writer demonstrates command of grade-appropriate conventions of standard English.				

Narrative

Traits	1	2	3	4
The writer establishes a situation, introduces a narrator and/or characters, and organizes an event sequence that unfolds naturally.				
The writer includes dialogue and descriptions of actions, thoughts, and feelings.				
The writer uses temporal words and phrases to signal event order.				
The writer provides a sense of closure to the narrative.				
The writer demonstrates command of grade-appropriate conventions of standard English.				

Key
1–Beginning
2–Developing
3–Accomplished
4–Exemplary

Comments

Opinion/Argument

TRAITS	1: Goal Oriented
The writer states a strong opinion, position, or point of view.	When I start an opinion piece, I state my opinion or point of view. I need to tell exactly what my view is. After reading this prompt, I can state my position as ____.
The writer supplies well-organized reasons that support his or her opinion using facts, concrete examples, and supporting evidence from the text.	I need to think of two or three good reasons to support my opinion. My opinion about this prompt is ____. I'll jot down the evidence I need to support my opinion. Then I'll go back to my writing and include them.
The writer links opinions and reasons using words, phrases, and clauses.	I need to link my reasons together using words and phrases, such as *for instance, in order to,* and *in addition.* I am going to look for places where I can add these words and phrases.
The writer provides a concluding statement or section.	When I finish writing an opinion piece, I need to finish with a strong statement that supports my whole argument. When I conclude this opinion piece, I can restate my position as ____.
The writer demonstrates command of grade-appropriate conventions of standard English.	I am going to read through my writing to make sure that I formed and used both regular and irregular verbs correctly. I will read through my whole opinion piece to make sure that I have spelled words correctly.

2: Directive and Corrective Feedback	3: Self-Monitoring and Reflection	4: Validating and Confirming
Reread the first sentences of your writing. Then go back and reread the prompt. Did you clearly state an opinion that answers the prompt? Revise your statement to make it clear and focused.	Tell me how you chose ____ as your opinion. How can you make your position clearer for the reader?	I can see that your position is ____. You made your opinion very clear. That got me to pay attention to the issue.
What are your reasons for your opinion? Find supporting details and evidence in the text for each reason. Group these ideas together in separate paragraphs.	How did you decide to organize your ideas? Did you identify the information that was most important to include? How did you do this?	You included some strong evidence to support your opinion.
Let's read this paragraph. I see a reason and some evidence. How can you link these ideas together? I notice that you have more than one reason to support your opinion. What words can you add to show the reader that you are moving from one reason to another?	Show me a part of your opinion piece where you link ideas using words and phrases. Show me a part where you could improve your writing by using linking words or phrases.	The words and phrases ____ and ____ are very effective at linking together the connection between your opinions and reasons. They help me understand your ideas.
Reread the last sentences of your opinion piece. Does it end by restating your point of view? Go back and look at your opinion statement. How can you reinforce this idea in your conclusion?	How does your conclusion support your opinion or the position that you have taken? Is there a way you could make this conclusion stronger?	Your concluding section clearly supports your point of view. You've really convinced me that your point of view makes sense.
Read that sentence again. Does it sound right to you? Your noun and verb don't agree. How should you edit that? When you write a title, what do you need to do?	Show me a place in your writing where you used compound and/or complex sentences. Show me a place where you used commas correctly. What rule of punctuation did you apply?	Your opinion piece included many compound sentences and you remembered where the commas should go. I noticed you spelled many difficult words correctly.

Informative/Explanatory

TRAITS	1: Goal Oriented
The writer introduces his or her topic with a main idea statement.	When I start an informative/explanatory text, I introduce my topic. I'm going to think about what I want my readers to know about ____. Then I create a main idea statement.
The writer uses facts, definitions, and details to develop his or her points.	I need to find facts and details from the text to support my points. I can go back to the text and underline parts that I think will help my writing. Then I will include them in my informative/explanatory text.
The writer groups related information together.	It is important that I group ideas together in an order that makes sense. I am going to categorize my information to help me structure the parts of my informative/explanatory text.
The writer uses linking words and phrases to connect ideas within categories of information.	I need to connect my ideas together using linking words and phrases, such as *another, for example, also,* and *because*. I am going to look for places where I can add these words and phrases.
The writer provides a concluding statement or section.	When I finish writing an informative/explanatory text, I need to summarize my ideas in a conclusion. When I conclude, I can look back at my main idea statement, then restate it as ____.
The writer demonstrates command of grade-appropriate conventions of standard English.	I am going to read through my writing to make sure that I capitalized each sentence as well as the proper nouns I've used.

I'm not sure I spelled the word ____ from the text correctly. I'm going to go back to the text and check the spelling. |

Common Core Writing to Texts Grade 4 • ©2014 Newmark Learning, LLC

2: Directive and Corrective Feedback	3: Self-Monitoring and Reflection	4: Validating and Confirming
How could you introduce your topic in a way that tells exactly what you will be writing about?	Take a look at your main idea statement. Do you feel as if it clearly introduces your topic?	Your main idea statement is clearly ____. That introduction helped me understand exactly what I was going to read about.
What are your main points? Find supporting details and evidence in the text for each point.	Have you included all of the facts you wanted to share about ____?	You included some strong facts, definitions, and details to support your topic.
Put your facts and details into categories. These categories can be the sections of your informative/explanatory text.	How did you decide to organize your ideas? Did you look at an organizing chart? How did it help you?	You organized your informative/explanatory text into [number] well-defined sections.
Let's read this paragraph. I see two related ideas. How can you link these ideas together?	Show me a part of your informative/explanatory text where you could improve your writing by using linking words or phrases.	The words and phrases ____ and ____ are very effective at linking together ideas.
Reread the last sentences of your informative/explanatory text. Do they restate your main idea?	Show me your concluding statement. Is there a way you could make this conclusion stronger?	After I read your conclusion, I felt I had really learned something from your writing.
Read that sentence again. Does it sound right to you? Your noun and verb don't agree. How should you edit that? Look at the word ____ in that sentence. Check your spelling.	Show me a place where you correctly used an irregular noun or verb. Where have you used an apostrophe correctly?	Your informative/explanatory text included many complex sentences. I notice you were very careful to check your spelling.

Narrative

TRAITS	1: Goal Oriented
The writer establishes a situation, introduces a narrator and/or characters, and organizes an event sequence that unfolds naturally.	I will use a sequence-of-events chart to jot down the events I will write about. I will record details from the text I have already read. I will include those details in my new narrative.
The writer includes dialogue and descriptions of actions, thoughts, and feelings.	I want to include descriptions in my narrative. I will write down words that will let my readers picture what I am writing about. Then I will include these in my narrative.
The writer uses temporal words and phrases to signal event order.	When I write a narrative, I need to use signal words so that my reader does not get confused. I will add words and phrases such as *first, then, the next day,* and *later that week* to help my reader understand the order of events.
The writer provides a sense of closure to the narrative.	I am going to reread the ending of my narrative to make sure that it gives the reader a feeling of closure. I need to concentrate on how the problem in the narrative is solved.
The writer demonstrates command of grade-appropriate conventions of standard English.	I am going to read through my narrative to make sure that I formed and used both regular and irregular verbs correctly. I am going to scan through my narrative to make sure I used end punctuation on every sentence.

Common Core Writing to Texts Grade 4 • ©2014 Newmark Learning, LLC

2: Directive and Corrective Feedback	3: Self-Monitoring and Reflection	4: Validating and Confirming
Think of events that will lead from the problem to the resolution. You've decided to write about ____. Now think of the sequence of events you will include.	What graphic organizer could help you organize your narrative events? Tell me how you went about organizing your narrative.	The events you organized lead to a [fun, surprising, etc.] resolution.
Imagine that you're a character. What's happening in the narrative? What do you have to say to other characters? What do you have to say about the events?	Show me how you gave information about your characters and setting.	I can visualize where your narrative takes place. You've included some nice descriptive details.
Let's read this paragraph. Is it clear to the reader when all the action is taking place? What words could you add to help the reader's understanding?	Show me where you used sequence signal words in your narrative. Show me a place where you could use signal words to make the order of events clearer.	The phrase ____ gave a nice transition between ____ and ____.
Let's read the ending of your narrative. Does it show how the problem is solved? Is there something you can add to make sure the reader feels like the narrative piece is over?	Show me how your ending gives the reader a feeling of closure. Are there any questions from the narrative that you feel were unanswered?	You've developed an interesting resolution to the problem in your narrative. It gives me a sense of closure.
I got confused about the sequence when ____. Take another look at your verb tenses. Make sure they are consistent.	Show me a place in your writing where your sentences could be better. What could you do to improve them? Show me a sentence where you changed the punctuation. How did you know it was wrong?	Your narrative included a lot of dialogue and you used punctuation correctly.

Editing/Proofreading Symbols

Mark	What It Means	How to Use It
	Delete. Take something out here.	We went to to the store.
	Change or insert letter or word.	San Francico, Calafornia my home.
#	Add a space here.	My familyloves to watch baseball.
	Remove space.	We saw the sail boat streak by.
	Delete and close the space.	I gave the man my monney.
	Begin a new paragraph here.	"How are you?" I asked. "Great," said Jack.
	No new paragraph. Keep sentences together.	The other team arrived at one. The game started at once.
	Transpose (switch) the letters or words.	Thier friends came with gifts.
≡	Make this a capital letter.	mrs. smith
/	Make this a lowercase letter.	My Sister went to the City.
	Spell it out.	Mr. García has 3 cats.
	Insert a period.	We ran home There was no time to spare
	Insert a comma.	We flew to Washington D.C.
	Insert an apostrophe.	Matts hat looks just like Johns.
	Insert quotation marks.	Hurry! said Brett.
?	Is this correct? Check it.	The Civil War ended in 1875.
STET	Ignore the edits. Leave as is.	Her hair was brown. STET